John Goddard

The Super Flies
of Still Water

with colour photographs by the author
and line drawings by Ted Andrews

A & C Black · London

Published in paperback 1989 by
A & C Black (Publishers) Ltd
35 Bedford Row, London WC1R 4JH

First published 1977 by
Ernest Benn Limited, London

Reprinted 1982

ISBN 0 7136 5677 8

A CIP catalogue record for this book
is available from the British Library.

Printed and bound in Great Britain by
St Edmundsbury Press Ltd
Bury St Edmunds, Suffolk

Contents

The Super Fly Selection   4

General Patterns   5

Imitative Patterns

Lures

The Super Fly Selection

The patterns chosen for inclusion in this book have, for the sake of simplicity, been divided into three sections. The first category I have decided to refer to as 'General Patterns', the second as 'Imitative Patterns' and the last as 'Lures', as this seems to be the popular choice of most modern stillwater anglers. For easy reference all dressings in each section are listed alphabetically. In an effort to cater for the many different styles of fishing, sufficient patterns have been included in each group to give as wide a choice as possible, and while it is not the purpose of this volume to recommend any particular style, I do feel that a short discourse on the three main methods is called for.

By far the oldest method was perfected in Scotland during the latter half of the last century. This is generally referred to as drift fishing and is practised from an open boat drifting with the wind and utilizing a team of wet flies fished downwind on a floating line. Whilst this method was undoubtedly perfected then, loch fishing for trout in Scotland with flies from a boat was certainly practised as far back as the sixteenth century, but the type of flies or precise methods used I have been unable to discover. As far as the second method is concerned, lure fishing as we know it today has certainly been a product of the post-war era. On the other hand basic lure fishing for trout, which encompasses trolling or the trailing of imitations of small fish, can be traced back for many centuries. One of the earliest accounts I have found concerns a learned gentleman who seems to have been connected with the church nearly 600 years ago, as he was originally referred to as 'the holy angler'. It seems that through the course of time this was changed to 'The Angler Hermit'. According to legend his skill as an angler was little short of miraculous and I should like to quote the following taken from a book published in the last century. 'Soon finding that the salmon frequenting the lake would not take any of the flies or lures such as worms or dead bait, he devised a most ingenious lure fashioned after the shape of a young trout, painted and coloured in such exquisite style as to deceive anyone, and certainly the salmon and trout which frequented the loch. This lure he trailed behind his light curragh, and many a lordly salmon and great trout fell by its allurement

4

to his prowess.' The third method, referred to as imitative fishing, which entails the use of artificials tied to represent the natural fauna on which trout feed, has mainly been developed in the last two decades. But let us not forget the great debt we owe in this respect to that fabulous fly fisherman the late Dr. Bell of Wrington in Somerset, who was undoubtedly responsible for the original concept of imitative fishing with such famous patterns as the Amber Nymph and the Blagdon Buzzer, to mention but two of the better known flies he perfected between the two wars on his beloved Blagdon Lake.

General Patterns

Perhaps suggestive patterns would be a more descriptive heading for artificials in this category, as most of them initially seem to attract trout by virtue of their general shape and colour, and then tempt them into acceptance because of their superficial resemblance to some form of aquatic life on which trout feed. All these artificials are traditional patterns that have been developed over the years. Several of them such as the palmer dressings can be traced as far back as the sixteenth or seventeenth centuries and their originators are lost in the mists of time. Without doubt I feel sure that in many cases their inventors based their originals on some specific form of aquatic or terrestrial life, but due either to the limited materials available to fly dressers up to the early part of this century or inaccuracies in interpretation of a dressing as it has been passed down over the years, possible attempts at imitation are not always apparent. Despite this several of them do bear an astonishing resemblance to natural fauna, but whether this was by design or accident has never been established. Certainly all dressings included in this category are very killing patterns under the right conditions, and have proved themselves time and time again over the years. Even today many of them are reserved a place of honour in my fly box.

One of their most important aspects is their very anonymity, which means many of them will at times be accepted by trout under any conditions of weather, depth of water or speed of retrieve. This is an extremely useful attribute as they can be used to explore a water if you are unable to ascertain on what the trout are feeding. Nevertheless to obtain the best results from each pattern its position on the leader and the way it is fished are still of paramount importance if the best results are to be obtained from the pattern.

Imitative Patterns

As the name implies most of the artificials in this category have been designed specifically to imitate a particular species of natural food on which trout feed, and to obtain the best results it is essential to fish these in a manner as close as possible to the naturals they are meant to represent. Most of these artificials are of fairly recent conception, as it is only in the last two decades since stillwater trout fishing has become so popular that increased interest and research has led to their development. No doubt the tremendous increase in bank fishing during this same period has also influenced designs, for it was soon realized that imitative patterns were more important in this respect. Prior to the middle of this century, and apart from fishermen on a few of the smaller lochs and larger reservoirs such as Blagdon, the majority of trout anglers fished from boats, drifting with the wind and fishing in the traditional Scottish loch style with a team of flies. In those days casting from an anchored boat was practically unknown, and general patterns were the order of the day. The choice of pattern is always of considerable importance no matter which type of fly is to be mounted, and although it is not the main purpose of this book to advise anglers in this respect I should like to emphasize that so far as imitative patterns are concerned the correct decision is essential. While most of the artificials in this group are close copies of the corresponding naturals a few vary in some respects as it has been found in practice that they can often be made more attractive to the trout by over-emphasizing certain anatomical features apparent in the natural or even its size or colour. In the same way exaggeration in movement when fishing them can often pay dividends, but this must be applied intelligently. For example when fishing a dry sedge, a very killing method on occasions is to retrieve it as fast as possible across the surface, much faster than the natural would normally move. This seems to excite the trout into taking, but this only seems to be effective in rough conditions or as dusk approaches. In a flat calm particularly during the day it is usually a waste of time, and is more likely to put the trout down than bring them up. In a further instance it is generally recognized that artificials to represent hatching midge pupae should be fished exceedingly slowly or even with no movement at all, yet on occasions a medium fast retrieve will induce fish to take. In fact on some waters for periods of days or even weeks I have known trout steadfastly to refuse a slowly retrieved pupa. At times of course trout become preoccupied feeding on one particular species of food, and it is during these periods that the angler who is able to present a corresponding artificial will succeed, where others may fail. On the other hand there are certain days on all waters when trout are really feeding well, when they will accept practically any pattern shown to them no matter how it is presented. These days are the exception and therefore the fly fisherman that has a good selection of patterns and knows how to present them will usually finish the season with a greater number of trout to his credit as well as a better average weight.

It will be noted I have not included any patterns to represent Mayflies, partly because of the considerable number of patterns to choose from and also due to the fact that apart from many of the Irish Loughs these large ephemerids are but rarely observed on still water.

Lures

The flies in this last category are much larger, being dressed on long shank, double or even treble hooks, and in many cases are highly coloured. A number of these lures were originally developed in the early part of this century from general patterns for sea trout fishing, and as stillwater fishing has progressed they have been readily accepted in this new environment, although most have been subjected to minor modifications. The majority of the bewildering variety available today, however, are the products of the modern stillwater angler. The forerunner of this new breed of lures was undoubtedly the Jersey Herd originated by that great stillwater trout fisherman T. C. Ivens. This new and rather revolutionary pattern created quite a sensation when it was first introduced and over the years it has certainly accounted for a lot of trout. While it is still an effective pattern it has to some extent now been superseded by even more killing artificials. A large percentage of these lures bear no resemblance at all to any type of natural food likely to be found in or on the water, and for several years now the question why trout accept them has been hotly disputed in the angling press. The possible explanations are so complex I do not intend to discuss them here, but there is no doubt at all that over an average season on most waters they account for a lot of trout. One reason for this is that lure fishing is a very popular part of the modern stillwater angling scene, and today the majority of anglers taking up this branch of our sport start off by fishing lures, as in many respects it is the simplest form of fly fishing and will provide the odd trout even for the tyro with little or no experience. On the other hand there are many experienced anglers who prefer this style of fishing, and although I personally only fish lures when the necessity arises I would be the first to admit that there is a lot more to it than just stripping back the lure as fast as possible. Make no mistake there is considerable art in this method, the speed and variation in retrieve, the depth at which the lure is fished as well as choice of pattern and type of fly line used. The modern lure fisherman is well catered for in this respect with slow sink, fast sink, sink tip and even lead cored lines to assist him in presentation. Unfortunately many anglers, even those that have been fishing for many years, never really develop this art, nor do they graduate to the other styles. I always think this is a great pity, for in my opinion much of the joy and excitement in fly fishing is encompassed in choosing the correct pattern and fishing it by the most effective method. I would also add that satisfaction in angling is further enhanced when most of the flies in your box have been dressed by yourself.

1 The Blae and Black

A traditional pattern, I have been unable to trace its origins but I understand it was a very popular sea trout fly in the larger sizes in Ireland during the early part of this

8

century. Between the wars, dressed on small hooks between 12 and 16, it gained a considerable reputation on lakes and lochs in Wales and Scotland. In these areas it is also known as the Duck fly. Like many of the early patterns it is of a rather sparse appearance, but let this not mislead you. It is a very killing artificial! A wet fly, it is reputed to imitate the chironomidae buzzer family of flies, but I doubt very much whether this was the intention of its originator. When it is tied in the smaller sizes, however, there is no doubt that it is a very passable imitation of the emerging pupae of many of the small dark buzzers or midges that hatch out in the early part of the season. To a large extent of course it has now been superseded by many of the more sophisticated midge pupae patterns that have been developed in the last decade or so, but I still feel it is worthy of a place in one's fly box, because it is so effective as a general pattern. It may be fished on the point or dropper in conjunction with a slow sinking or floating line with a medium to slow retrieve, while from a boat it is most effective dribbled along the surface on the top dropper. In my opinion it is best fished just in or under the surface and there is no doubt it kills best during March, April and early May.

A fairly simple pattern to tie, the dressing is as follows. Tie in at the bend to form the tail four or five golden pheasant tippets followed by flat or oval tinsel. The body material is then tied in and although my preference is for black wool, floss silk or seal's fur may be used as an alternative. The body should be dressed thicker towards the shoulder and this is then ribbed with the tinsel. The hackle of soft black hen (2 or 3 turns) is then tied in behind the eye and finally the wings of medium starling are tied in on top of the hackle and sloping back. A small black cock hackle may be utilized in place of the hen hackle on very tiny patterns as this is easier to tie.

Dressing

Hook	D/E size 12 to 16
Silk	Black
Tail	Golden pheasant tippets
Rib	Flat or oval silver tinsel
Body	Black wool
Hackle	Black hen
Wings	Medium starling

2 The Black Zulu

Despite extensive research I have been unable to trace the originator of this pattern. Certainly it has been an extremely popular and killing fly for very many years, particularly on the Irish and Scottish lochs, where it was used extensively in the latter half of the nineteenth century. Tom Stewart points out that it bears a distinct resemblance to a Dove pattern created by Charles Cotton some 300 years ago, so it could well be a development of this. Even if this proves to be incorrect, I would point out that the palmer method of tying in the hackle, which is the basis of this pattern, can be traced back to the earliest days of fly fishing. Traditionally it is supposed to represent various species of aquatic beetles, and some of our earlier authorities suggest it should be fished well sunk close to weeds or the margins of lakes. I must admit it could well prove most effective where aquatic beetles are observed, for like most of these the fly itself is predominantly black, and there is no doubt the flat silver ribbing appears to be a good representation of the small silvery bubbles of air which are to be seen on the body of the natural. Fished in this way I would suggest the size of the artificial would be important, and should match the size of the natural beetles as closely as possible.

Other authorities state this pattern is best fished from a drifting boat in the traditional Scottish loch style, mounted either on the middle or top dropper (bob). This was an extremely popular pattern fished in this manner on many Scottish lochs, Welsh lakes and North Country reservoirs during the early part of this century.

The Black Zulu is one of my favourite flies when drift fishing, I love to dribble it along the surface in the bob position, and personally I find it most effective in the early part of the season. Retrieved in this manner it probably appears to a trout like a freshly hatched fly either in difficulties or trying to escape.

A fairly simple pattern to dress, the procedure is as

follows. A short tag of bright red wool is tied in at the bend, followed by flat silver tinsel, which is left hanging to be wound over body and hackle later. The body of black seal's fur or wool should then be applied thickening towards the shoulder or eye of hook. Personally I prefer black ostrich herl. Finally a black cock hackle of the appropriate size should be tied behind the eye and wound palmer fashion down the body to the bend. The hackle is held in position by the silver tinsel which is now ribbed back over it to the eye where a whip finish with the tying silk completes. The hackle should be wound fairly sparsely, and care should be taken when ribbing not to trap too many of the fibres.

Dressing

Hook	D/E size 10 to 14
Silk	Black
Tag	Bright red wool
Rib	Flat silver tinsel
Body	Black seal's fur, wool or ostrich herl
Hackle	Black cock. A hen hackle may be used for patterns to be fished to represent any of the aquatic beetles.

N.B. To make the pattern extra buoyant for fishing on the bob, I usually tie in an extra black cock hackle behind the eye. It may also be of interest to note that the original dressing specified black silk for the body and a black hackle with a touch of green in it.

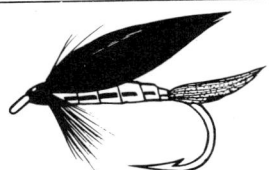

3 The Butcher

There are several variations of this pattern such as the Bloody, Gold or the Kingfisher Butcher, but it is the original that has achieved world wide fame, in fact H. P. Henzell states in his book *The Art and Craft of Loch Fishing* that if he was ever placed in the desperate position of being restricted to one fly only this would be his choice. Personally I would not go as far as this, but without doubt it is a most effective general pattern fished under the right conditions. The originators of this splendid fly in the early

11

part of the last century were apparently two gentlemen, hailing from Tunbridge Wells, by the names of Moon and Jewhurst, but it was not until the early part of this century, when loch fishing became popular, that its name became really established. There is no record that it was ever intended as a specific imitation of anything, but in practice I have found it is accepted most readily in the early part of the season when various species of chironomidae are the predominant item on the menu of the trout. Fished just under the surface it bears a resemblance to the pupa of the orange and silver midge, which has bright silver body segments with orange-red or often bright red body segments. In the past most authorities advised that this pattern dressed on a fairly large hook should be mounted on the top or middle dropper, and although some suggested it was more effective fished on the point, they all agreed it was best used on the drift from a boat, just in or under the surface. In fact a special split winged pattern of this fly was developed specifically for fishing on the top dropper or bob, and there is no doubt that it was effective. Whilst I have caught trout fishing with it in this manner, there are in my opinion other patterns much more suited to this style of fishing. Today this fly is most effectively deployed by the bank fisher in the smaller sizes 12, 14 or even 16 and should be retrieved at a medium to slow pace fairly deep during the day or near the surface morning or evenings utilizing either a floating or sink tip line.

The Butcher is a fairly simple pattern to dress once you have mastered the art of tying in wings. Commence by tying in the tail or tag of red ibis (as an alternative you may use a small section of white feather dyed bright red), proceed with the body material of wide silver lurex which is then wound tightly up to the eye, where a black hen hackle is added. The wings, which should be tied in sloping back, are formed from paired sections of quill feathers of blue black crow, or alternatively rook or magpie may be utilized.

Dressing

Hook	D/E size 10 to 16
Silk	Black
Tail	Red ibis
Body	Wide silver lurex (varnished for long life)
Hackle	Black hen
Wings	Crow quill

4 The Coch-y-Bonddu

Typical of many of the general patterns listed in this section, the Coch-y-Bonddu is an excellent all rounder, and seems to be equally effective fished either wet or dry. This is a very old pattern and it has been difficult to trace its origin. I have ascertained, however, that an artificial referred to as the Welshman's Button or Hazel Fly was well known in the seventeenth century; the dressing is so similar I have little doubt that the present day pattern is a development from it. The first reference I found to this early pattern is in a late seventeenth century book called *The Angler's Museum* by Thomas Shirly, while the same dressing is also listed in that well known book of the same period, *The Art of Angling* by Thomas Best. The dressing they give is a body of mixed peacock and ostrich herl with a black hackle, and red wings from a partridge tail. During the latter part of the seventeenth and early eighteenth century the dressing was slightly modified, with a furnace hackle replacing the black hackle and red wings, and this is how it appeared in Ronalds' *The Fly-Fisher's Entomology*, dated 1836. He also prefixed the name Marlow Buzz. All these authorities seem to agree that this pattern was originally tied to represent the Coch-y-Bonddu, Bracken Clock, or June Bug (*Phyllopertha horticola*) as it is known in different areas. This is a species of beetle common in both Wales and Scotland, where it is to be observed amongst fern or bracken. A terrestrial species, they are often blown onto waters in considerable numbers on windy days throughout the month of June. Their bodies and legs are black, the thorax metallic green, while the wings are reddish brown. When these or similar species of beetle are on the water, the artificial should be fished on the top dropper just in or under the surface. As previously mentioned this is also effective fished wet on a sinking line, and like many of these old patterns may be used throughout the season. It is interesting to note that this was very popular as a wet fly on rivers throughout the last century.

An easy pattern to dress, the first step is to tie in a short length of red or orange floss (or fine gold tinsel or wire). This is used to rib the body, which is formed from two strands of herl from near the eye of a peacock feather. This should be tied in thickening towards the shoulder, and is then ribbed with the floss. Finally a furnace cock hackle (red with black tips) is tied in sloping back over the body. Use four turns if a semi buoyant fly is required, but only two turns for a pattern to be fished wet. Some of the older dressings suggest a small tag of red or white wool.

Dressing

Hook	D/E size 8 to 12
Silk	Brown
Rib	Orange or red floss silk
Body	Bronze green peacock herl—2 strands
Hackle	Furnace cock with black tips

N.B. With the present shortage of good furnace hackles an acceptable alternative is to tie in a small black cock hackle, one to two turns, followed by a large red cock hackle, two to three turns.

5 The Dunkeld

This is typical of many of the traditional patterns which have been popular for many years. There seems little doubt that it was developed, though modified, from the salmon fly of the same name, but by whom or when I have been unable to discover. Neither have I been able to trace the originator of the salmon fly, though it would appear to have been perfected over a very long period as a similar dressing is mentioned by Francis Francis in *A Book on Angling* first published in 1867. Initially it was probably developed for sea trout fishing, but it was as a lake or loch fly that it eventually gained fame. Most authorities seem to look upon it as an attractor pattern and state that as such it should always be fished on the point, where, it was generally agreed, it probably emulated a small fish. Whether or not they were correct is immaterial as it seems to be a very killing pattern however it is fished. One of my favourites, it has over the years provided many fine trout, but strange to relate I have never enjoyed much success with it fished as a tail fly. Personally, in common with many of my acquaintances, I now always fish it on the middle dropper and I find it equally successful from either boat or bank. In practice it seems more effective retrieved at a slow to medium pace, and will take trout at any level. I would also suggest that it kills far better in the latter half of the season.

A slightly more difficult pattern to dress, the first operation is to tie in at the bend a tail of golden pheasant crest followed by a length of fine gold wire, a cock hackle dyed hot orange and finally a length of flat gold tinsel. This is then wound closely along the shank to the eye and secured with the silk. Follow with the hot orange hackle wound palmer style to the eye and secure with the silk. The fine gold wire is then wound through the hackle over the body to the eye, and tied in. Then tie in the wings of brown mallard speckled shoulder plumage; these should slope well back down the body. Finish off with a small jungle cock or substitute tied in on each side at the eye.

Dressing

Hook	D/E size 10 to 12
Silk	Black
Tail	Golden pheasant crests
Ribbing	Fine gold wire
Body	Wide gold tinsel or lurex
Wings	Brown mallard speckled shoulder
Hackle	Hot orange cock tied palmer style
Cheeks	Small jungle cock eye feather or substitute

6 Greenwell's Glory

Without doubt this must be one of the most successful and popular flies ever devised, and furthermore it is equally beloved by both river and stillwater fishermen, who fish it either in its wet or dry form. In fact it is one of the few flies which has become almost a legend, and is consequently known outside trout fishing circles. Despite this it is not such a popular fly today as it has been in the past, as it is after all a general pattern, meant to represent any of the olive duns or their nymphs, whereas now most anglers tend to choose patterns to represent specific species.

The history of this fly has been well documented, and the basic facts are as follows. Whilst the name of the fly perpetuates the Durham Canon whose surname was Greenwell, the credit for the pattern should really go to his fly dresser, one James Wright of Sprouston, a professional dresser of flies. One day in May, so the story is told, the Canon brought to Wright an olive dun that he had caught on the water that day and asked him to dress a pattern to represent it. Apparently Wright's copy was so successful that it was duly christened and immortalized by the Canon. Even so some doubt as to the true originator still exists, as a dressing recommended by one Mark Aitken several years before is extremely similar. Originally the Greenwell was fished and dressed as a wet fly, but as dry fly fishing became increasingly popular the pattern was slightly modified and became a great favourite, from the swift and rocky rivers and streams of the north to the gentle placid chalk streams in the south. It was also used extensively and gained a rapid reputation on many lakes and lochs, where it was dribbled gently over the surface on the top dropper as a bob fly. As far as the modern stillwater fisherman is concerned it is still a very useful pattern to have in one's box, to be fished in this way to represent either hatching pond or lake olives. In its original form as a wet fly it is also a useful general pattern, and may be fished at various depths either from a slowly drifting boat or better still from the bank to represent any of the nymphs of olives on stillwaters where they are observed.

Like many of the older traditional fly patterns it is fairly simple to tie. First of all tie in a length of fine gold wire with yellow tying silk, which should then be well waxed before winding back to the eye to form the body. The next step is to rib the body with the gold wire and then tie in two or three turns of a Coch-y-Bonddu cock hackle. The final operation is to tie the paired wings of blackbird over the top of the hackle and sloping well back. According to the original dressing these should be split to finish, but this is rarely practised nowadays. On the other hand the wings for the dry pattern which are tied in before the hackle is applied are well split with a figure of eight tying and should be raked well forward over the eye (see page 15).

Dressing

Hook	Size 12 or 14
Silk	Yellow
Body	Yellow silk with cobblers' wax applied to give body a greenish-yellow hue
Rib	Fine gold wire
Hackle	Coch-y-Bonddu cock
Wings	Blackbird tied in and split, sloping back for the wet pattern or forward for the dry

7 The Grenadier

This is one of those excellent patterns devised by that great stillwater angler Dr. Bell of Wrington. Most of his fishing was pursued on Blagdon reservoir in Somerset between the wars, where he gained a reputation as an accomplished angler of considerable vision. I think it would be true to say that he was largely responsible for the first positive attempts to design artificial patterns to represent some of the many forms of aquatic life found in still water. Several of his dressings have survived over the years and are still popular and in use today. This particular pattern however is something of an enigma, for while I feel sure he originally intended it as a copy of some specific species, the secret must have died with him since I have been unable to trace any written records. For this reason I have decided to include it in this section of general patterns, and possibly this was his intention anyway. In general outline it is very similar to many of the old traditional style of spider-type dressings so beloved by most wet fly fishers on many of our north country rivers. It is very lightly dressed and I believe the venerable doctor used to fish it well sunk. Today it is generally accepted that it will succeed fished at any depth, even on occasions as a semi-dry fly fished just in the surface. I find it is more effective in the latter half of the season, and prefer to fish it on the dropper. Retrieved slowly on a slow sink line it has provided me with some nice trout, particularly on those hot, calm days in mid-summer when little seems to be moving on the surface.

An extremely simple pattern to dress. To start with tie in at the bend a length of oval gold tinsel with which to rib the body. This can be either hot orange floss or seal's fur and should be tied in from the bend, thickening towards the eye or shoulders. Finally tie in a light furnace cock hackle (two turns only) and complete with a whip finish.

Dressing

Hook	D/E size 13
Body	Hot orange floss or seal's fur
Rib	Oval gold tinsel
Hackle	Two turns of light furnace cock

8 The Grey Duster or Parachuting Badger

I have been unable to trace the precise history of this fly other than to substantiate that it originated somewhere in the northern part of Wales. It owes its popularity over the years to the late Courtney Williams, who publicized full details in his famous book *A Dictionary of Trout Flies*. According to this he was first introduced to the pattern by local anglers fishing on the Alwen, a small mountain stream running into the Dee. He was so impressed with the performance of this fly on the many waters subsequently fished that he stated it was perhaps the best general dry fly of all, and at one period it apparently tempted him to become a one-pattern angler.

As far as the stillwater angler is concerned I doubt that the original dressing is as popular as it used to be a few years ago, as there are now so many specialized patterns available. However, Preben Torp Jacobsen, the well known Danish fly dresser, apparently discovered that by replacing the normal hackle with a horizontal (parachute) hackle it proved to be even more effective, particularly on still water, and he calls his dressing very appropriately the Parachuting Badger. This is no doubt due to the preference of most trout in still water to feed mainly in or under the surface film rather than on top, that an artificial dry fly dressed in this manner would probably appear to be more normal. Certainly it is a good general dry pattern to try, particularly in the evenings when trout are dimpling the surface and you are uncertain on what they are feeding. It is also an excellent standby through June and July when the large hatches of caenis are experienced, for dressed on a tiny hook it is one of the few patterns that will take the odd trout under these often infuriating conditions. In conclusion I can do no better than to quote the words of one of our leading fly fishers who states 'This fly seems to have the ability to induce trout to rise when nothing else will'.

The original dressing is very simple to tie, but I have decided to give Preben Torp Jacobsen's pattern. This incorporates the parachute hackle which is to be favoured for still water, and requires a certain amount of expertise in construction. To start with, a short length of stiff hackle stalk or monofilament is whipped with brown tying silk in the centre of the hook shank. This stem should protrude about half an inch vertically. The tying silk is then wound down to the bend where the body material is tied in, being a dubbing of light rabbit's fur with or without a touch of the blue under-fur. It should be wound evenly along to the eye where it is whip finished. It is now only necessary to tie in the black and white badger hackle parachute style. To accomplish this whip on the hackle behind the eye, take along the top of the body and wind around the stem (two or three turns). Strip off excess flew and take the bare stalk back to the eye and whip finish. Finally trim off excess of protruding vertical stem and administer a small blob of varnish. There are several other methods of dressing the parachute hackle, but this is the one I prefer.

Dressing

Hook	U/E size 12 to 15
Silk	Brown
Body	Light rabbit's fur with or without a touch of the blue under-fur
Hackle	Cock badger tied parachute style

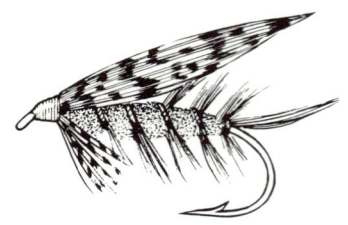

9 Invicta

This fine pattern was apparently invented by James Ogden towards the end of the eighteenth century. One of the foremost fly dressers of his period, he played a major role in the development of both the dry fly and eyed hook. A keen observer of nature, it has been suggested that he produced the pattern specially for lake and loch fishing, and with his known reputation I think this a fair assumption. There is no direct evidence to suggest he ever intended this as an imitative pattern. I suspect otherwise, however, for it is certainly a very fair representation of a hatching sedge fly.

A great favourite with older generations of fly fishers in the early part of the century, the Invicta was renowned as a killing pattern. Even today it is still extremely popular, and with the proliferation of patterns now available to the modern fly fisher, this speaks for itself. You will always find a few of these in my own fly box dressed on size 12 and 14 hooks, as I find it an excellent stand-by when drift fishing from a boat. As a general pattern it will take the odd trout throughout the season fished at any level, but in my own experience it is most effective fished just in or under the surface from early June onwards. Dressed on the smaller sized hook it should be fished on the middle dropper, or on the top dropper or bob position with the larger hook. I must admit this latter method is my favourite. Dribbling it along the surface in the traditional Scottish loch style can be most rewarding and exciting. I use it fairly extensively throughout June during the early hatches of sedge-flies, but later on in the season, once the really heavy hatches commence, I discard it in favour of specific sedge patterns.

Although this may appear to be a rather complicated pattern to dress it is in fact fairly simple if the following directions are adhered to. Commence by tying in the tail fibres of golden pheasant crest feathers, then secure the length of oval gold tinsel for ribbing the body. The body dubbing of yellow seal's fur is next wound up to the eye,

where a red game cock hackle is whipped on, and wound
back down to the tail sparsely. This is then secured with the
tinsel, which is ribbed back over the body and through the
hackle to the eye. Next tie in a throat hackle from the wing
of a blue jay, and trim off the top section to make room
for the wing formed from the flew of a hen pheasant centre
tail. This should be tied in along the top of body, sloping
well back.

Dressing

Hook	D/E size 10 to 14
Silk	Brown
Tail	Golden pheasant crest feathers
Rib	Oval gold tinsel
Body	Yellow dyed seal's fur
Body Hackle	Red game cock tied in palmer fashion but sparsely
Throat hackle	From wing of blue jay
Wings	From hen pheasant centre tail

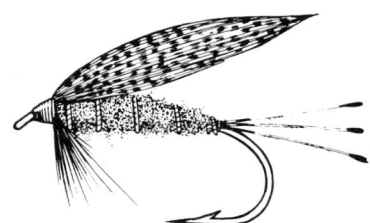

10 Mallard and Claret

This is certainly the best known and most popular general
pattern of all, and has literally dominated the scene since
the early days of loch fishing. Despite this its origins seem
to be in some doubt. In his book *A Dictionary of Trout
Flies*, Courtney Williams admits to this, although he does
state it is generally attributed to one William Murdock, a
one time celebrated Aberdeen fisherman and fly dresser
who is said to have evolved many first class lake flies,
including the well known Heckham Peckham. He does
however inform us that it is not a particularly old pattern. I
would query this as in *A Book of Angling* written by Francis Francis and published in 1867 a list is provided of dressings (unnamed) of Scottish lake flies that had apparently
been popular for many years. Among this list a dressing is
given which apart from any mention of a tail of golden
pheasant tippets is so close to the pattern we use today that

21

it strongly indicates this is a much older artificial than has been generally supposed. I think the omission of tail feathers by Francis Francis was an oversight, for in a book written many years before by W. C. Stewart called *The Practical Angler* you will find a list of materials recommended for loch flies including most of those used in a Mallard and Claret, and Stewart states quite clearly that all large loch flies are improved by adding a tail of a few fibres of the feathers taken from the neck of a golden pheasant. A very similar dressing is also to be found in a book called *The Moor and The Loch* by John Colquhoun published in 1840.

Described by many as the sheet anchor of the stillwater angler, this is a fine pattern and can be relied upon to produce results throughout the season. Although I am sure it was never intended to represent any particular insect, it is, with its rather drab colouring, suggestive of many forms of aquatic life. It is therefore a good pattern to try if you are uncertain on what the trout may be feeding, or when on a strange water. The smaller sizes seem to be more effective early in the year, but I favour the larger sizes from July onwards. It should be fished slowly rather than fast, and it seems equally effective from both bank or boat and at any level in the water where the fish happen to be feeding. Most authorities seem to favour fishing it on the point, but I have always found it more effective when fished from a dropper.

Once you have mastered the art of winging a fly, the tying of this pattern should present no problems. The first operation is to tie in about six short golden pheasant tippets to form the tail, using black tying silk. Then add a length of fine gold wire to rib the body, which is formed from very dark claret seal's fur. This should be wound on thickening towards the shoulders. Next wind on the ribbing and tie in your hackle of white cock dyed claret. Finally the wings of dark bronze mallard are tied in on top and sloping well back. I prefer a dark claret hackle, while some fly dressers seem to favour a dark red cock or even a black hackle.

Dressing

Hook	D/E size 10 to 14
Silk	Black
Tail	Golden pheasant tippet feathers
Rib	Fine gold wire

Body   Dark claret seal's fur
Hackle Claret or natural red cock
Wings Dark bronze speckled feathers from a
           mallard

11 The Peter Ross

Also an extremely popular and well known pattern, it was at one time regarded as the most killing lake fly throughout the country. This pattern was evolved in the early part of the century by one Peter Ross, an extremely competent fisherman who owned a small general store in Killin, Perthshire. No fly dresser himself, he is reputed to have taken a Teal and Red, a popular lake fly of the period, to a local dresser and suggested several improvements. The new pattern proved to be far superior and quickly gained a reputation locally, where it soon became known by the name of its originator. In the past it was generally reputed to represent the freshwater shrimp, but why this should have been I really cannot understand, as it bears little resemblance. In latter years it seemed to have been accepted as a good imitation of most small fry likely to be encountered in still water, and it is in this context that I have always used it. Most authorities seem to agree that it is one pattern that should always be fished on the point, well under the surface on a sinking line. While I favour this method for most conditions, I must point out that during July and August, when the large shoals of sticklebacks and other small fry venture forth from the heavy weed growth or margins in very shallow water, a floating line with the leader degreased should be used. Under these conditions you can fish your fly just under the surface and work your way casting along the shoreline from the bank, or from a boat if you have a friend with you to manoeuvre it. This pattern should always be fished fairly fast with frequent jerks and pauses.

    To dress this pattern start by tying in several golden pheasant tippet feathers for the tail, and follow these with a length of thin oval silver tinsel for ribbing the body. This is followed by a length of flat fairly wide tinsel or silver lurex, which forms the first third of the body. For the remainder of the body it is best to use bright red seal's fur, although some dressers use red wool. The next operation is to rib the body with the fine silver tinsel and tie in a black hen hackle at the throat. Finally, use the breast feathers of a teal duck to form the wings, tied in on top and sloping well back.

Dressing

Hook	D/E size 10 to 14
Silk	Black
Tail	Golden pheasant tippets
Body	Tail half flat silver lurex remainder bright red seal's fur
Rib	Fine oval tinsel
Hackle	Black hen
Wings	Breast feathers of a teal duck

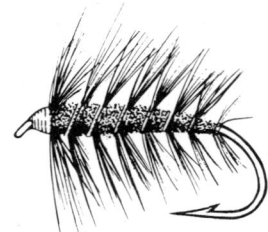

12 The Red Palmer

While this may not be the most famous or popular of all the patterns listed in this book, it certainly has the honour of being the oldest. In fact the palmer method of hackling a fly can be traced back to the earliest periods of fly fishing history, because the original list of twelve artificial flies given in *The Treatise of Fishing with an Angle* included a pattern called the Block Louper, which was dressed in this fashion. Various palmer patterns were very popular in the sixteenth and seventeenth centuries, and in those days they were generally referred to as palmer worms as apparently they were originally meant to represent various species of caterpillars. It would seem that the Red Palmer originally developed from a pattern listed in *Angling Improved*, published in 1706, and it is surprising how closely the dressing as it appears in this ancient volume compares to the one we are most familiar with today. The only difference is in the material used for the body, which throughout the sixteenth and seventeenth centuries is always given as peacock herl. It is interesting to note some authorities still suggest this. The first reference I can find to the red body as now preferred appears in a book by William Blacker published in 1855 called *Flymaking Angling and Dying*, where he refers to this pattern as the Soldier or Red Palmer. In the early part of this century it was probably the most popular fly with Scottish loch fishers, particularly with the majority of anglers in those days who fished a team of flies on a short line from a boat in the traditional loch style. While it may be fished wet on a sunk line, where it will take the odd trout, it really reigns supreme fished as a bob fly on the top dropper from a boat. It is one of the few general patterns that I use consistently from early June onwards. I only use it when drift fishing from a boat, and dribbled along the surface on the top dropper it certainly accounts for a lot of trout. Some authorities suggest it is also a good pattern to fish dry in the evenings, but personally I prefer to use the modern more imitative patterns.

It is a very simple pattern to dress, and is an excellent fly for the novice fly tyer to start with. Tie in at the bend a length of oval gold tinsel for ribbing the body, and then wind in the dubbed body of red seal's fur or wool. This should be dressed thickening to the shoulder, where a red cock hackle is tied in. This should be a large hackle as it has to be wound palmer fashion over the body down to the tail. It is then secured with the gold tinsel which should be ribbed back up the body through the hackle to the eye, where it is secured by the silk with a whip finish. Any hackles trapped under the ribbing may be eased out with a dubbing needle.

Dressing

Hook	Size 8 to 12
Silk	Red
Body	Red seal's fur or wool
Hackle	Large natural red cock

13 Silver March Brown

A well known pattern, which was particularly popular with loch fishermen between the wars. It was originally developed for sea trout fishing, probably in Ireland, and is but a variation of the March Brown itself, one of the best known and oldest patterns of all. In fact Cotton in *The Compleat Angler* gives a dressing that is recognizable, as did Chetham in his *Angler's Vade Mecum* published in 1681, where it was referred to as the Moorish Brown. I am sure whoever was responsible for the original dressing of the silver variation did not intend it as a specific representation of any living creature. Consequently it was looked upon as a general pattern in its early days and a jolly good one too. In recent years some authorities have suggested it is a fair representation of the freshwater shrimp, and should be fished on the point near the bottom in shallow water, where these crustaceans abound. Although it will take the occasional trout when it is fished in this manner, I can really see little resemblance to the natural in the dressing. Most other authorities state it is a good fly to fish in the evenings when sedges are hatching, and I do subscribe to this point of view, because in the water it certainly bears more than passing resemblance to a hatching sedge. While it may be fished from the bank, I prefer to use it mounted on the dropper when drift fishing from a boat. I well remember my first 4½ pound brown trout many years ago from Blagdon, which came to this pattern on one of those bright sparkling mornings, which often seem characteristic of this most beautiful of waters early in the summer. During the day, fish this pattern slowly on a well degreased leader, but when the sun is low on the horizon, grease the top part of the leader and retrieve it a little faster just under or in the surface.

A straightforward pattern to dress, it should give even the tyro little trouble. The tail of two or three fibres from a brown speckled partridge hackle or tail feather is tied in, followed by a length of fine silver tinsel for ribbing the body. This may be formed from flat wide silver tinsel or lurex, or alternatively you may form the body from dubbed hare's ear ribbed closely with the lurex, which is my personal preference. Next tie in the hackle of mottled brown partridge, and finally the wings, of mottled hen pheasant secondary wing feathers. These should be tied in on top, and sloping well back to the bend of the hook.

Dressing

Hook	D/E size 10 to 14
Silk	Brown
Tail	Two or three fibres from a brown speckled partridge hackle or tail feathers
Rib	Fine silver tinsel
Body	Wide flat silver tinsel or lurex
Hackle	Mottled brown partridge
Wings	Mottled hen pheasant secondary wing feather

or for variation

Rib	Wide silver lurex
Body	Dubbed hare's ear, closely ribbed with silver lurex

14 Teal and Green

The Teal series have always been popular general patterns with the stillwater angler, and were considered indispensable by the old Scottish loch fishers, particularly the red variety, which was widely used in the latter half of the nineteenth century. It was supposed to be an excellent representation of the freshwater shrimp. All the patterns in this series look alike apart from the colours of the body and hackles, which were many and varied. The series can be traced back to the beginning of the nineteenth century, and it would seem that they were one of the earliest artificials to be developed specifically for fishing in the Scottish lochs. It is interesting to note that W. C. Stewart in his book *The Practical Angler* published in 1857 gives a list of materials to be used for flies for loch fishing, and these include all those in common use today for this series, except that mohair was suggested in place of seal's fur.

Of the many colours in this series the Teal and Green is now one of the most favoured, and although it is a pattern I seldom use myself, it is undoubtedly a useful fly to have in one's possession, as it is one of the few artificials with a green body. It should be looked upon purely as general pattern, and according to many experts it should be fished deep and fairly fast. It is best fished on a dropper, and is equally effective from both boat and bank.

The procedure for dressing this pattern is similar to most of the general flies already listed. To commence, tie in two or three fibres of golden pheasant tippet, and follow with a length of oval silver tinsel for ribbing the body. The body of dubbed green seal's fur is then wound towards the eye, leaving plenty of room to tie in the hackle of natural red hen, which, as with most of these wet patterns, should be finished by taking several turns of silk diagonally over the front and top of the hackle to ensure it is flattened on top and pointed towards the rear. We are now ready to tie in the wings, formed from teal breast or flank feathers. The latter are bigger and more suitable for larger flies.

Dressing

Hook	D/E size 8 to 14
Silk	Black
Rib	Silver oval tinsel
Tail	Golden pheasant tippet fibres
Body	Green seal's fur
Hackle	Natural light red hen
Wings	Teal breast or flank feathers

15 Teal Blue and Silver

I am including this pattern with the Teal and Green as it is one in the same series. Although like all the others the Teal Blue and Silver was first developed for loch fishing, it was as a fly for sea trout that it received great publicity. But it has remained popular with lake or loch anglers, with whom it still enjoys a certain reputation. While it is looked upon as a general pattern and should be used as such, many consider that because of its gay colouring it should be classified as a lure or attractor pattern. But as it is smaller than the average lure it is a useful in-between fly, and with its bright dressing it may be used with advantage when the water is discoloured after heavy rain or when there is heavy algae bloom present, which often occurs after a prolonged period of bright sunny weather. It should be fished on the point, retrieved fairly fast, and is usually more effective when fished on a sinking or sink tip line.

The procedure for dressing this pattern is the same as for the Teal and Green—only the materials differ.

Dressing

Hook	D/E size 8 to 14
Silk	Black
Rib	Fine oval silver tinsel
Tail	Golden pheasant tippet fibres
Body	Wide flat silver tinsel or lurex
Hackle	Hen dyed bright blue
Wings	Teal breast or flank feathers

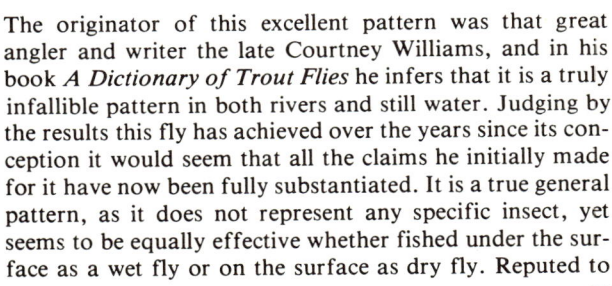

16 The Welsh Partridge

The originator of this excellent pattern was that great angler and writer the late Courtney Williams, and in his book *A Dictionary of Trout Flies* he infers that it is a truly infallible pattern in both rivers and still water. Judging by the results this fly has achieved over the years since its conception it would seem that all the claims he initially made for it have now been fully substantiated. It is a true general pattern, as it does not represent any specific insect, yet seems to be equally effective whether fished under the surface as a wet fly or on the surface as dry fly. Reputed to attract the larger trout, results seem to confirm this, so it most assuredly deserves a place in one's fly box. A spider pattern, it is double hackled, which probably accounts for its success when fished as a dry fly. When floatant is applied it floats extremely well for long periods.

Tom Stewart, the well known Scottish fly dresser, had a high opinion of this pattern and mentioned in his booklet *Fifty Popular Flies* that Fred Irving, four times champion of the Greenock and District Angling Club, achieved outstanding success with this fly, often when other anglers were finding it difficult to catch a single fish. While it is normally dressed on size 12 or 14 hooks he found it was far more effective dressed on a size 16, and recommended that it should be fished on the point very deep in the colder months of the year, and near the surface in the warmer months under calmer conditions. This is a pattern that should always be retrieved slowly, preferably with frequent pauses.

A simple pattern to dress, it is another fly ideal for the beginner to start on. The tail or whisks of two strands from a partridge's tail are tied in at the bend, followed by a length of fine gold tinsel for ribbing. The body of dark claret seal's fur should be wound on evenly and not too thickly and then ribbed with the tinsel. This pattern has two hackles and the first to be tied in is a white cock hackle dyed dark claret; this is followed by a slightly larger snipe rump feather, close up to it and nearest the eye of the hook. A dark partridge back feather may be used in place of the snipe.

Dressing

Hook	D/E size 12 to 16
Silk	Black
Tail	Two strands from a partridge tail
Rib	Fine gold tinsel
Body	Dark claret seal's fur
Hackles	Rear: a white cock dyed dark claret
	Front: a snipe rump feather or feather from back of partridge

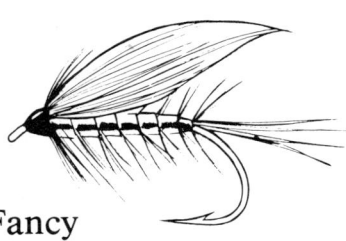

17 Wickham's Fancy

No list of general patterns would be complete without this popular and well known pattern. It is reputed to have been invented by a Dr. T. C. Wickham, a well known angler in the Winchester area in the early part of this century. It was apparently developed from a much older pattern called the Cockerton. The doctor asked a local fly dresser to tie some of these and gave him the dressing from memory. The directions proved to be incorrect, but the resulting fly was so successful he gave his name to it. Other authorities state it was evolved many years before in 1884 and was first tied by a professional fly dresser, one George Currel of Winchester, from a design given to him by a Captain John Wickham. Whoever was responsible it has proved to be a very successful pattern, and has accounted for many trout over the years. A fancy fly, it does not represent any particular insect, so its main attribute is as a general pattern, and in this context it is certainly useful. Not only is it equally effective when fished in any position on the leader, but it can be fished at any depth or at any time throughout the season. While it is normally fished as a wet fly, the late Courtney Williams states it is more effective when dressed and used as a dry fly, particularly in the smaller sizes for smutting fish, but as it is a pattern I seldom use dry I am unable to substantiate this view.

To dress this fly proceed as follows. For a start, tie in several fibres from a red game cock hackle for the whisks or tail. Next tie in a length of fine gold wire, followed by a length of wide flat gold tinsel or lurex which should then be ribbed around the hook shank two thirds of the distance to the eye. The body hackle of red game cock is then wound palmer-wise down to the bend, taking care to wind it between the gold ribbing. This is secured with the fine gold wire which is then wound back through the hackle towards the eye and secured by the thread with a whip finish. A further red game cock hackle is then tied in at the throat, and the final operation is to tie in the wings of dark starling wing quill on top and sloping well back. If you intend to fish this pattern predominantly as a dry fly it will be necessary to tie in an extra throat hackle. It is also worth noting that some anglers omit the wings, as it is considered by many to be more effective as a hackled pattern.

Dressing

Hook	D/E size 12 to 16
Silk	Yellow
Tail	Red game cock fibres
Rib	Fine gold wire
Body	Wide flat gold tinsel or lurex
Body Hackle	Red game cock tied palmer fashion
Throat Hackle	Red game cock—two for dry pattern
Wings	Starling wing quill or grey duck wing quill for larger size

Imitative Patterns

18 The Adult Midge

One of my own patterns, which was developed specifically to represent the adult chironomid after it has hatched and is active on top of the surface film. A few years ago it was most unusual to find trout regularly engaged feeding upon the adult chironomid, or midge, as they are commonly called. During the past two or three seasons the pattern has changed, and now on many bodies of still water it is not at all uncommon to observe trout feeding upon the adult to the exclusion of anything else. It is therefore very necessary to have an appropriate pattern to offer the trout at this time. Why the trout have recently become addicted to the adult I have been unable to ascertain with any certainty, but I suspect it may be due to a change in the behaviour of the midges. In the past the adults were seldom observed on or near the surface for any length of time once they had hatched, but now either after hatching or at a later stage they may be observed flying slowly over the surface for long periods. When so engaged their legs trail in the surface film creating a perceptible V shaped wake, and it is at this time that the trout intercept them as they pass overhead. When the trout are rising to these adults they are very difficult to catch, because if your artificial is stationary they will ignore it, and conversely if it is fished too fast the excessive wake will scare them. This pattern should always be fished on the point, and if possible it should be mounted on a long rod with a light line and very long leader. If there is a little breeze it can then be dapped lightly on the surface. This seems to be the most successful method and is particularly effective at or near dusk. I dress this pattern in three basic colours—green, orange and black—and tie them in two sizes.

This is an extremely simple and quick pattern to dress and is ideal for the novice to start with. Using yellow silk tie in a length of fine silver tinsel at the bend, and then after waxing the silk, twist on your body material of seal's fur in the chosen colour. The body should be dressed full, because after the seal's fur is tied in it can be picked out with a needle to simulate the legs of the natural. Next rib the body with the tinsel and finally tie in a dozen or so strands of white bucktail or polywing yarn across the body with a figure of eight finish, to represent the wings. Cover the roots of the wings with more seal's fur.

Dressing

Hook	D/E long shank, size 12 or 14
Silk	Yellow
Body	Olive green, orange or black seal's fur
Rib	Fine silver tinsel
Wings	White bucktail

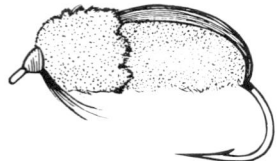 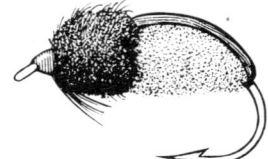

19 The Amber Nymph

It would be hard to find a more rewarding nymph pattern with which to open this section. The Amber Nymph is one of the earliest imitative artificials specifically designed for lake fishing. The originator was the famous Dr. Bell of Wrington, one of the few well-known anglers of his period who specialized in stillwater trout fishing. A thoughtful and farsighted fisherman, there is no doubt he was largely responsible for the first movements towards the present day highly developed techniques. He created several excellent imitative patterns but most of them have now been superseded by similar artificials that have been evolved by the use of more sophisticated and modern materials. The Amber Nymph, however, is probably still as popular today as it ever was. Originally invented by Dr. Bell in the early part of this century for fishing his beloved Blagdon, its fame soon spread, and it is now one of the better known flies in general use on many still waters throughout the country. Although there is no written evidence to substantiate what particular aquatic insect it was meant to imitate, there is little doubt in my mind that he intended it to represent many of the species of sedge pupae that are predominantly of an orange-brown colouring. According to information that has been passed down over the years, the venerable doctor favoured a large pattern for the early part of the summer, followed by a smaller one for later in the season which incorporated a minor variation in the dressing. Most authorities suggest the artificial tied on the larger hook should be used from April to the end of June, and the smaller from then on. Although I do not use this pattern so frequently nowadays, at one time it was a great favourite of mine, and then I seldom used it before the beginning of June. Usually fished on the dropper, it should never be retrieved too fast, and while it is effective fished at any level in the water, I have found it accounts for most trout when presented near the surface. It will take fish throughout the day from the bank, particularly in the shallow areas, but it is best fished from a boat during the evenings.

The only differences between the two patterns are in hook sizes (hook 12 or 13 for the small or 10 or 11 for the larger) and the colour of the thorax. Commence with a strip of any grey-brown feather for the wing case, which is tied in at the bend of the hook. Follow this with the body material of amber yellow seal's fur, which should be tied in thickly, and next take the wing case material over the top of the body and tie in. Follow with seal's fur for the thorax, very dull brown or black for the large pattern and hot orange for the small. Finally tie in the legs composed of a few fibres of a honey hen hackle. These are tied in immediately behind the eye of the hook, sloping backwards under the thorax.

Dressing

Hook	D/E size 10 or 11 large, size 12 or 13 small
Silk	Black (large), yellow (small)
Wing Cases	Fibres of any grey brown feather, tied in over top of body
Body	Amber yellow seal's fur
Thorax	Dark brown or black (large), hot orange (small)
Legs	Honey hen hackle fibres, tied in sloping back under thorax

20 The Black and Peacock Spider

One of the earliest post-war patterns produced specially for stillwater fishing, it was first introduced and popularized by the well known reservoir fisherman T. C. Ivens. Over the years it has become an increasingly popular artificial, and although it is often used as a general pattern I have decided to include it in this section, as it is also a good representation of several forms of aquatic life. This pattern can be used by the fisherman with confidence throughout the season and seems to be equally effective fished either near the surface or close to the lake bed. It should always be retrieved slowly. A very fair representation of many species of aquatic beetles, it often proves to be effective fished well below the surface near the margins or in the vicinity of weed beds where most beetles are likely to be found. I have also found it a useful pattern fished dry on the surface on those odd occasions when terrestrial beetles are blown onto the surface in numbers. Tom Ivens informs us in his classic *Still Water Fly Fishing* that he has found this pattern particularly deadly during the evening rise when the trout are head and tailing very slowly. At this time the trout are often moving barely a foot below the surface and therefore it is essential that the black and peacock spider is fished 2 to 6 inches below the surface and retrieved very, very slowly to prevent any perceptible wake, which would scare the trout. To keep your fly fishing at the right depth, it will be found necessary to grease the leader, except for the last 18 inches in front of the artificial. It is also reputed to be a good pattern to use when trout are feeding on the smaller varieties of aquatic snails. These are often blackish-brown tinged with green, which the peacock herl body of this pattern matches almost to perfection. This is usually during the warmer weather of mid summer

36

between late June and early August when some species float to the surface and remain there for some time. It is hardly surprising, therefore, that I have personally found this pattern to be most effective at this time fished very slowly sink and draw.

This is a popular pattern with the amateur fly dresser as it is a quick and simple pattern to dress. With black tying silk secure three or four strands of bronze peacock herl, followed by a length of dark floss silk. Wind the floss up the shank thickening towards the eye and tie in. Next twist the strands of herl together in an anti-clockwise direction, and wind up to the eye in a clockwise direction and secure. Finally tie in a relatively large soft black hen hackle by the stub, with the underside of the feather facing the bend. Take two turns only and tie off.

Dressing

Hook	D/E size 8 to 12
Silk	Black
Underbody	Black floss silk
Body	Three or four strands of bronze peacock herl
Hackle	Soft black hen

21 The Chompers

Developed and perfected by Richard Walker in the early 1970s this pattern tied in different colours has proved to be exceptionally killing and has consequently accounted for a lot of large trout. In a similar manner to the Black and Peacock Spider it should really be looked upon as a general pattern, but again in its various colours it bears more than a passing resemblance to a corixa, freshwater shrimp, louse or a sedge larva. This is a pattern that should always be fished slowly, either in small jerks on a sinking line along the bottom, or on a floating line utilizing the sink and draw method. I have found the white chomper fished by this latter method particularly effective on those bright calm days when few trout seem to be moving. At this time the take is just as likely on the sink as on the draw, so therefore it is important to watch the line carefully for any unusual movement. On small waters where distance is unnecessary I usually watch the leader, but on large reservoirs where distance is sometimes more important I watch the loop of line hanging down from the rod tip. I normally fish this pattern alone on the point of a long leader, as it seems to be less effective when fished as one of a team of flies.

Also a very simple pattern to dress, it is especially suitable for beginners as it is quick and easy to tie yet has a very lifelike appearance when completed. Cover the shank in the usual manner with brown tying silk and then at the bend tie in a piece of raffene (synthetic raffia made of viscose) followed by three or four strands of dyed ostrich herl in the desired colour to form the body. These strands should be twisted together in an anticlockwise direction and then wound along the shank. It is then only necessary to dampen and stretch the raffene over the top of the herl body and tie down at the eye. If a more lengthy body is desired the loose end of the raffene tied in at the bend may be tied back down the shank with the silk. Some fly dressers may be tempted to varnish the raffene back of the completed fly, but this should be resisted, for it will prevent it absorbing water, and it is the absorbed water which gives the artificial its translucency.

While this pattern may be dressed on very large or very small hooks, Richard has found the most useful sizes appear to be 10 and 12. He also suggests that the amber coloured pattern is sometimes more effective when dressed with buff coloured raffene.

Dressing

Hook	D/E size 10 or 12
Silk	Brown, black or olive
Body	Three or four strands of ostrich herl, dyed amber or olive or natural white
Wing Case	A strip of brown raffene

N.B. For a more durable pattern the tying silk along the shank should be varnished before winding on the body material.

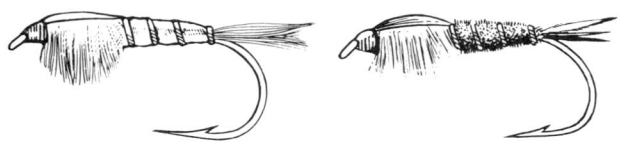

22 Collyer's Green and Brown Nymphs

These two most lifelike patterns were devised some years ago by that master of the art of fly dressing, David Collyer. Since then they have become increasingly popular and have proved to be the downfall of many a large trout. Unlike most trout flies, these patterns were not brought about by a gradual process of evolution, but as David freely admits were the result of one evening's work. Dissatisfied with most standard nymph patterns available at the time, he spent one afternoon in a boat on Weir Wood reservoir in Sussex netting natural nymphs. These were then duly transported home to his fly tying bench where the above dressings were perfected within a matter of hours, from the naturals under magnification. These are not meant to be specific representations of any particular natural nymphs, but rather a generalization of many nymphs found in both running and still water. As a result they have proved to be effective on all types of water from the big reservoirs to small northern becks. This is another pattern that should always be fished by itself on the point preferably in conjunction with a floating line.

On still water it is best fished in the vicinity of weed beds where natural nymphs abound. As a slow retrieve is favoured takes are often very gentle so the line or leader should be watched carefully at all times. Unlike most nymph patterns this one is unweighted, so it is a useful artificial to have in one's box for those conditions where a very slow sinking variety may be desirable.

A rather tricky pattern to dress, it should not be attempted until a degree of experience has been achieved. The method of dressing the green nymph is as follows. Tie in rib of oval gold tinsel at bend and then follow with three or four strands of olive-dyed goose or swan herl with the tips protruding beyond the bend to form the tails. Wind the herl up the body for about two-thirds of its length and tie in, then rib with three or four turns of the oval tinsel. Next tie in the olive-dyed ostrich, and wind forwards and backwards along the remaining third of the hook shank to form the thorax. Finally tie in the olive-dyed goose or swan at the eye; this is then doubled and re-doubled over the thorax to form the wing case. The dressing for the brown nymph is the same, but different coloured materials are used as listed.

Dressing

Collyer's Green Nymph

Hook	D/E size 10
Silk	Olive
Rib	Oval gold tinsel
Body and Tail	Three or four strands of olive-dyed goose or swan herl
Wing Case	Olive-dyed goose or swan herl
Thorax	Olive-dyed ostrich herl

Collyer's Brown Nymph

Hook	D/E size 10 or 12
Silk	Brown
Rib	Olive gold tinsel
Body and Tail	Three or four strands of cock pheasant centre tail
Wing Case	Cock pheasant centre tail
Thorax	Chestnut-dyed ostrich herl

23 Corixa (Plastazote)

Typical of the new breed of stillwater patterns which have dominated the post war angling scene, this artificial utilizes a revolutionary modern material (plastazote) which has introduced a new concept to the techniques of stillwater trout fishing. I have been unable to ascertain with any certainty who first introduced this material, despite various enquiries, although it could well have been Dennis Stowe of Chingford. Richard Walker, who was largely responsible for popularizing it, informs me that he was first introduced to it by this gentleman. That well known professional fly dresser David J. Collyer was responsible for the original dressing of this particular pattern. With its extremely buoyant body it can be fished in a completely different way from traditional patterns. Fished on the point in conjunction with a fast sink or Hi D line it will float on or near the surface depending on the depth of water and length of the leader, but as soon as the retrieve is commenced it will dive towards the bottom imitating the natural corixa to perfection. It will be appreciated that this artificial works in the opposite way to a traditional weighted corixa fished in the sink and draw style, which means under certain circumstances it may prove more attractive to the trout.

Although these buoyant flies are not difficult to dress, they are rather time consuming. First of all cut a small rectangular block of plastazote to the appropriate size and then slit it half way through with a razor blade. Alternatively a hole may be pierced through the centre with a hot needle. Then wind your tying silk thickly along the shank of the hook, apply a liberal coating of glue, and push the block over or onto the shank with the slit uppermost. The weight of a book or similar object is sufficient to keep the block in place till the glue has set. The body can then be snipped to the desired shape with a sharp pair of scissors. The brown feather fibres should then be tied in at the bend and brought tightly over the top of the body and whipped in at the eye. Two pheasant tail fibres may then be tied in, one each side of the eye to simulate the paddle shape legs or oars of the natural beetle. It is also a good idea to tie in two or three close turns of silver tinsel at the bend behind the body to imitate the tiny silvery bubble of air collected by the natural at the surface. If plastazote is not obtainable polyethylene, which is similar but a little coarser may be used as substitute for the body.

Dressing

Hook	D/E size 10 or 12
Silk	Brown
Body	Shaped section of plastazote
Back	Brown feather fibre (dyed goose or cock pheasant centre fibre).
Oars	Two pheasant tail fibres

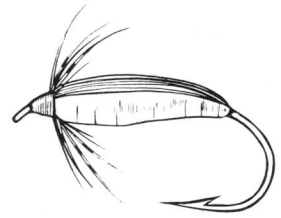

24 Corixa

The various species of natural corixidae which this pattern represents are very common in all types of water, and although they are a staple diet of trout at certain times of the year, they are often only taken when other more succulent forms of food are in short supply. This is not a new artificial. Leonard West recommended a dressing to represent them in the early part of this century, although it should be pointed out this was intended to be fished in running water. The earliest record I can trace of a dressing intended specifically for still water is a pattern perfected by C. E. Walker and detailed in his book *Old Flies in New Dresses*. Since then many dressings have appeared and the one I have chosen is I hope representative of most of them. It can be dressed as a weighted or unweighted pattern. On most reservoirs and lakes the best time of the year to fish this artificial is from mid-July to mid-September. During the day I have found the weighted pattern to be more effective fished on the point with a floating line and retrieved by the sink and draw method. In the very early morning or late evening there is no doubt that the unweighted pattern is more killing, for when the light is poor the trout become bolder and chase the corixa into very shallow water. At this time the artificial should be retrieved fairly fast just under the surface. A good compromise which sometimes seems to be effective is to fish the weighted version on the point with the unweighted one on a dropper.

If a weighted pattern is required, copper wire or strip lead should be wound around the shank of the hook. Then proceed in the following manner for both patterns. With brown tying silk tie in at the bend a bunch of brown squirrel tail fibres, followed by a length of fine silver wire, and white floss. The floss is then wound down to the eye, full in the centre to give a well tapered body. This is then ribbed with the wire, and the squirrel fibres are stretched over the top of the body to form the wing cases and whipped in at the eye. Finally six fibres from a grouse hackle are tied in under the eye, sloping well back under the body. To prolong the life of the very fine squirrel tail fibres, it is a good idea to apply a dab of varnish at each end.

Dressing

Hook	D/E size 10 or 12
Silk	Brown
Body	White silk floss
Rib	Fine silver wire
Wing Cases	Bunch of squirrel tail fibres
Throat Hackle	Six fibres from a grouse hackle

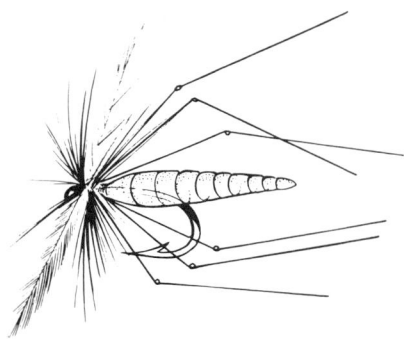

25 Daddy Longlegs

The largest member of the Diptera Order, there are many different species and the natural flies are often also referred to as crane flies. There is little doubt that these large insects have attracted the attention of anglers and fly dressers since the very early days of fly fishing and doubtless many patterns have been evolved to represent them. However the earliest dressing I have been able to trace that mentions a pattern suitable for reservoir fishing is in Leonard West's well known book *The Trout Fly* which was published in the early part of this century. The natural fly has long been used for dapping, and even today it is still used on many of the Irish loughs as it was during the last century. There are now many artificial patterns with little to choose between them, as most of them seem to take trout when the naturals are on the water in sufficient quantity to tempt them. I do have a preference, however, for a pattern devised by the well known professional fly dresser Geoffrey Bucknall, in which the special plastic body used gives it a most lifelike appearance. This fly was designed to provide a true dry fly version of the Daddy for bank fishing in place of the hairy things often used for dapping. The fly is cast to rising trout, and it does not drown easily as would a dapping fly when thrown a long way from the bank. This pattern should be well treated with floatant prior to use, and then cast out and left to lie without movement in the vicinity of rising fish. Fished in this manner during July and August when the naturals are blown onto the water in fair numbers it will take trout when other artificials are completely ignored. This method has also proved to be productive from an anchored boat. Apart from dapping the only other method that will sometimes tempt the odd trout is to fish it during breezy days from a drifting boat on the top dropper in the traditional Scottish loch style. One word of warning—when using this pattern allow plenty of time before setting the hook, as a quick strike seldom produces results.

This looks like a complicated pattern to dress, but in practice it is fairly straightforward, even though a little time consuming. With brown tying silk tie in the special detached plastic mayfly body (this may be obtained from Veniards). Halfway along the shank of the hook next tie in the two hackle points to form the wings. These should be tied in the spent position, but sloping back slightly to the bend. The six strands of black nylon or horsehair are then knotted in the middle and three are tied in each side under the body and just behind the eye, sloping back towards the bend. A fairly thick hackle of up to six turns of a light red cock hackle is then formed.

Dressing

Hook	U/E size 10 or 12
Silk	Brown
Body	Special plastic detached mayfly body tied in about halfway along shank
Wings	Light ginger hackle points
Legs	Six strands of black horsehair or nylon
Hackle	Collar of light red cock hackles—six turns

26 Damosel Nymph

This is another pattern that is typical of the many completely new artificials that have appeared in the last two decades. As far as I have been able to ascertain the earliest dressing to specifically represent the natural nymph appeared in that excellent volume *Lake and Loch Fishing* by Col. Joscelyn Lane, first published in 1955. Since then many different dressings have been suggested most of which at some time or other I have tried. As a result one particular pattern emerged which proved over the years to be more effective than any of the others. This is a dressing that was perfected in the late 1950s by my old friend Cliff Henry, the well known amateur fly dresser. This, therefore, is the one I have decided to list. The natural damosel nymphs can be imitated successfully by the fly fisherman during two periods of their life cycle. In the early part of the summer, when they are immature, their movements among the weed and detritus on the lake bed tend to be laboured, and can be successfully imitated by an artificial dressed on the smaller sized hook, retrieved very slowly on a sinking line along the bottom. As maturity approaches they become more active and their fast, wriggling movements among the weeds are all but impossible to simulate. The second and probably the best opportunity occurs when the mature nymphs ascend to the surface, and swim, usually just under the surface, towards the shoreline, where they seek emergent vegetation, rocks or stones on which to dry out and hatch into the adult, fully-winged insect. This is usually in the morning or early afternoon during June or July, and at this time the standard pattern tied on the larger sized hook and retrieved in a series of long steady pulls just under the surface on a floating line is often surprisingly effective. Just how effective has been proved on many occasions. In fact on the day this pattern was first tested at Chew valley lake in the early sixties it produced a superb deep silver bodied rainbow of just over 5lb on a flat, calm, blazing hot day when little else was caught.

This is a most satisfying pattern to dress, and if tied neatly is most lifelike. Commence by tying in at the bend the tips of three olive cock hackles to represent the breathing filaments, which on the natural are tail-like appendages. Follow these with a length of flat gold tinsel, and then spin sufficient medium olive seal's fur onto the tying silk to form the body. This is then wound two-thirds of the way along the hook shank, thickening towards the eye, followed by the ribbing of flat gold tinsel, and there they are both tied in. The thorax material of dark olive brown seal's fur is then wound onto the remaining third of the hook shank and tied in at the eye. This is followed by the wing cases of brown mallard shoulder feathers which are doubled and redoubled over the thorax before being tied in at the eye. Finally reverse the hook in the tying vice and tie in a bunch of about six grouse hackle fibres, just behind the eye and sloping backwards, to represent the legs of the natural.

Dressing

Hook	D/E long shank size 8 to 12
Silk	Green
Tail	Tips of three olive cock hackles to extend $\frac{3}{8}$ inch beyond bend.
Body	Medium olive seal's fur, tapering to tail for two thirds of hook length
Rib	Flat gold tinsel
Thorax	Dark olive brown seal's fur
Wing Cases	Brown mallard shoulder feather fibres doubled and redoubled
Legs	Bunch of about six fibres from grouse hackle

27 Damosel Wiggle Nymph

I have included this as an alternative to the standard pattern, for although it is a more difficult and time-consuming artificial to dress it may well prove to be worthwhile, since by design it certainly has a more attractive action in the water. While this is one of my own original creations, I must point out that the basic principle of the hinged body was first brought to my attention in an American book on fly dressing innovations by Swisher and Richards. They suggest this hinged principle for tiny river nymphs, which quite frankly I thought was of dubious value, but I immediately felt sure that it was an idea that could be adapted very successfully for much larger nymphs and larvae, particularly for the nymphs of the damosel fly which required a built-in wiggle. Over the years most stillwater fly fishermen have realized that one of the most difficult forms of underwater life to imitate is this wriggling action of the damosel nymph as it swims along. Now while I do not suggest that this new artificial duplicates this action, it does, if retrieved intelligently with frequent pauses, impart a definite undulating movement which seems to be very attractive to the fish. I would also mention that as this book goes to press I have been experimenting with a tiny alloy plate whipped at an angle under the eye of the fly which looks like a miniature version of the diving vane on the front of an artificial plug (wobbler). This now gives this new pattern a fabulous wiggling action and I am eagerly awaiting the coming season to test it on the trout.

The method suggested by the American authors for dressing the detached tail section of this pattern is rather complicated, and after some experimenting I stumbled across a much simpler and more effective procedure. Dress your tail section in the normal manner on a standard hook of the appropriate size and when completed remove from the fly tying vice and with wire cutters snip off the complete bend of the hook as close under the three tails as possible. This can now be hinged onto the main body at the bend, utilizing the eye and a length of fuse wire which is looped through it and then whipped onto the shank of the main body hook. To complete the fly it is then only necessary to complete the body in the normal way. The procedure for dressing is so close to the standard pattern already detailed that I do not feel it is necessary to repeat.

Dressing

Hook	D/E size 8 to 12
Silk	Brown
Tail	Tips of three olive cock hackles to extend $\frac{3}{8}$ inch
Body	Olive seal's fur
Rib	Flat silver tinsel
Thorax	Dark olive seal's fur
Wing Cases	Three strands from a brown dyed turkey tail feather, doubled and redoubled
Legs	Bunch of olive hen hackle fibres

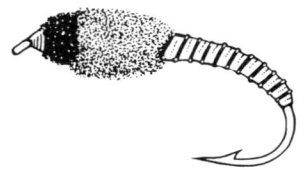

28 Footballer

This is another pattern devised by that notable professional fly dresser Geoffrey Bucknall, and with due respect I would suggest any pattern perfected by him be given careful consideration. The rather odd name given to this artificial came about from the appearance of the body of the original dressing which was formed from alternate strands of black and white horse hair, reminiscent of a footballer's jersey. First introduced many years ago at Blagdon it quickly accounted for many large trout and just as rapidly gained a reputation as a killing pattern. Whilst it was originally intended to roughly represent the pupae of the chironomid (midge) family, it was never intended as an exact representation, since one of the favourite fishing techniques of its originator during a midge or buzzer rise is to cast as quickly and as close as possible to a rising trout. When utilizing this technique it is desirable to get the fly through the surface film and in front of the trout's nose as rapidly as possible, so anything that might stick in the film was left out in favour of a clean penetrating outline. This is why for this particular pattern no attempt was made to add materials to represent the breathing tubes or emerging wings or legs. The original pattern was dressed with a black and white body, but it is now available in a wide range of colours to match the considerable variation to be found among the naturals. Due to the method of presentation this pattern should always be fished alone on the point of a long leader, which should be greased down to within six inches of the artificial. When it is cast out in front of a rising fish, a few seconds should elapse before the retrieve is made. This should be one steady pull, and if no hook-up is experienced, the line can be stripped back in preparation for a cast to the next rising trout. Once the cast has been made considerable concentration is necessary, as the trout is just as likely to take the artificial as it is sinking as on the retrieve.

An extremely simple pattern to dress, the first step is to wind white tying silk down the shank and well round the bend of the hook, where two strands of horsehair, one

1 Blae and Black

2 Black Zulu

3 Butcher

4 Coch-y-Bonddu

5 Dunkeld

6 Greenwell's Glory

7 Grenadier

8 Grey Duster

9 Invicta

10 Mallard and Claret

11 Peter Ross

12 Red Palmer

13 Silver March Brown

14 Teal and Green

15 Teal Blue and Silver

16 Welsh Partridge

17 Wickham's Fancy

18 Adult Midge

19 Amber Nymph

20 Black and Peacock Spider

21 Chompers

22 Collyer's Green and Brown Nymphs

24 Corixa

25 Daddy Longlegs

26 Damosel Nymph

27 Damosel Wiggle Nymph

28 Footballer

29 G and H Sedge

30 Gerroff

31 Hawthorn Fly

32 Hatching Midge Pupa

33 Lake Olive

34 Longhorns

35 Ombudsman

36 Pheasant Tail Nymph

37 PVC Nymph

38 Red or Green Larvae

39 Sedge Pupa

40 Shrimper

41 Small Hatching Midge

42 Snail (Floating)

43 Tadpolly

44 Walker's Sedge

45 Ace of Spades

46 Appetizer

47 Aylott's Orange

48 Baby Doll

49 Black Bear's Hair

50 Black and Orange Marabou

51 Church Fry

52 Jack Frost

53 Missionary

54 Muddler Minnow

55 Polystickle

56 Persuader

57 Sinfoil's Fry

58 Sweeny Todd

59 Whisky Fly

60 Worm Fly

Some Important Natural Species

Emerging Sedge Pupa

Damosel Nymph

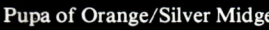

Pupa of Orange/Silver Midge

Adult Sedge Fly

black and one white, are wound side by side two thirds of the way up the shank to form the body. Mole's fur is then dubbed in to form the thorax followed by a single strand of bronze peacock herl, given a few turns to form the head.

Dressing

Hook	D/E size 10 to 18
Silk	White
Body	Black and white horsehair
Thorax	Natural mole's fur
Head	Single strand of bronze peacock herl

N.B. Black and clear monofilament may be used in place of the horsehair, which may be difficult to obtain in a good quality. Coloured variations may be obtained by winding clear nylon over fluorescent floss of the chosen colour with matching thorax of teased out fluorescent wool.

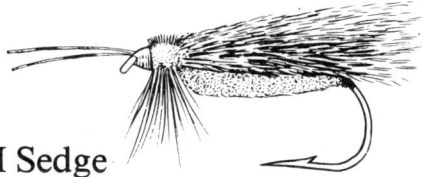

29 G and H Sedge

This pattern was devised by myself and my colleague Cliff Henry, the distinguished amateur fly dresser, many years ago. Its rather odd name is devised from the first letters of our respective surnames. Both of us were, and incidentally still are, particularly fond of fishing sedge patterns on still water either as a dry fly floating on the surface, or dribbled along on the top dropper from a drifting boat. While there were plenty of patterns to choose from at the time, they left much to be desired as they all lacked one or other of the two main features we felt necessary and considered essential in a really satisfactory pattern. These were a lifelike silhouette as seen by a trout from underwater, plus the ability to float high in the surface film for long periods without re-greasing. No such pattern existed, hence the appearance of the G and H Sedge which has since proved its value time and time again. The secret of its success is undoubtedly the deer's hair used to represent both body and wings of the natural, as this is probably one of the most buoyant of all materials available to the fly dresser today. From the bank, I have found it is most killing if used on its own on the point of a very long leader (at least 18 feet) with a floating line, and cast in the path of rising fish. It should then be allowed to lie without movement, when the trout usually take it very confidently. Sometimes the trout may appear a little reluctant to accept it, and then a slight tweak on the line as the trout swims past will often elicit an immediate response. In rough weather both from a boat and from the bank, a very rapid retrieve, almost skating it over the surface will often provoke a savage response from the trout. This is most exciting fishing particularly when the fish are really in a feeding mood. On the other hand there is little doubt in my mind that it is as an attractor on the top dropper from a drifting boat that it reigns supreme. Over the years, fished in this way, it must have provided us with hundreds of trout. From June onwards dribbled along in this manner in a good breeze it seems to attract trout like a magnet, and even in very rough conditions it seldom needs re-greasing. It is interesting to note that this is now a popular and successful pattern in America.

Unfortunately this is a difficult and time-consuming pattern to dress, and should only be attempted by the proficient fly dresser. After winding the green tying silk down the hook shank to the bend, tie in a doubled length of the same silk, to be used later for the underbody. The main body material of deer's hair is then spun onto the shank, starting at the bend and working down towards the eye. Several spinnings of this hair will be necessary, pressing each new one close up to the last until one arrives at the position where one has a hook completely palmered with the deer hair. (This is spun on in the same way as for a Muddler Minnow.) The hair should then be clipped with sharp scissors removing all the hair underneath and part way along each side, but tapering towards the eye to give the correct sedge silhouette when viewed from underneath. Two rusty dun cock hackles are then tied in together at the eye, leaving the stripped butts protruding over the eye to simulate the two antennae of the natural sedge fly. The top of this hackle is then trimmed. Finally dark green seal's fur (or any other desired colour) is twisted in between the double length of green silk which was originally tied in and left hanging at the bend. This is then pulled taut under the trimmed deer hair body and whipped in at eye.

Dressing

Hook	U/E long shank, size 8 to 12 ·
Silk	Green
Body	This is formed from several bunches of stiff deer hair—spun on and trimmed to shape
Underbody	Dark green seal's fur
Hackle	Two rusty dun cock, trimmed off on top

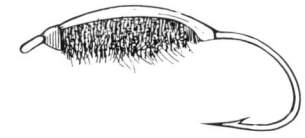

30 Gerroff

This is a new pattern that I devised originally for river fishing, to combat the peculiar conditions which applied during the height of the '76 season, when we were affected by the worst drought for more than two centuries. At this time the flow on the upper Kennet where I regularly fish was reduced to a crawl. Normal weighted nymph patterns were not very effective, therefore, as on this almost still water they sank too quickly. On the other hand, unweighted patterns were even less effective, for as a result of the general lack of surface fly, all the trout were feeding on or close to the bottom. I therefore came to the conclusion that a special pattern was required. One that would sink, but very, very slowly and at the same time look like an item of food to the trout. I decided on a shrimp pattern as being generally attractive to most fish, and to achieve the slow rate of sinking apart from using a buoyant material I only used half the length of the hook shank on which to dress the body. This did solve the problem and in addition had the added attraction of providing me with a pattern that presented a small silhouette, yet a relatively big hook to hold a large trout. Whether or not it was the size or appearance of the pattern or the materials chosen to dress it I do not know, but it certainly proved to be one of the most successful patterns I have ever devised. On its very first outing it accounted for two limit bags of 12 trout for two rods totalling 49lb, and since then has accounted for many other heavy bags from both rivers and still water. As far as still water is concerned I would not recommend it for large reservoirs or deep waters but for small relatively clear waters it is exceptionally killing. Mounted alone on the point with a floating line it should be cast out either in the

51

vicinity of a trout you can see feeding underwater, or alongside weed beds where trout are likely to be feeding. The plop of entry as it hits the surface will often attract fish from several yards and as it slowly sinks you can usually watch your quarry swim up, intercept and inhale. So confidently do trout accept this fly that many times I have watched small unwanted trout swim up and take it in their mouth, chew on it, spit it out and then take it again. On at least a dozen occasions I have observed a trout accept it and reject it three and even four times. In fact it was due to this that it received its rather peculiar name. I was fishing at the time with the celebrated stillwater angler, Brian Clarke, who was kindly testing out this new pattern. The water we were fishing was stocked with more than its fair share of small trout, consequently Brian spent most of the morning pulling the fly out of their mouths and shouting 'Get Off'. By lunch time this had become abbreviated to 'Gerroff' and he insisted in future it be known as such.

It is an exceptionally easy pattern to tie, and is ideal for the beginner. With brown tying silk tie in a narrow strip of PVC half way down the hook shank. Next mix olive brown seal's fur with some fluorescent pink (three parts olive to one pink) and spin onto the silk in an anti-clockwise direction, this should then be wound onto the shank in a clockwise direction up to the eye, with a slight taper at each end. To complete stretch the PVC over the top of the body material and tie in at the eye.

Dressing

Hook	D/E size 10 to 14 slightly longer shank than a standard hook
Silk	Brown
Body	Olive brown and fluorescent pink seal's fur mixed—three brown to one pink
Wing Case	Strip of PVC. (Note that the new latex material may be used in place of the PVC.)

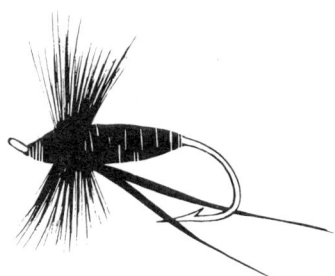

31 The Hawthorn Fly

This is a very old pattern and became very popular with river fly fishers in the latter half of the last century. Many of these river patterns are equally suited for stillwater fishing, and I was therefore faced with a difficult decision as to which particular pattern to recommend. After careful consideration I came to the conclusion that the most effective pattern I had ever tried was one sent to me by that master of the art of fly tying, the well known and respected Danish amateur fly dresser, Preben Torp Jacobsen. The natural fly is a terrestrial species which is to be seen on the wing between late April and early May. Under windy conditions particularly during mating these large black flies with their long trailing legs are often blown onto the water, sometimes in considerable numbers. When this happens the trout usually feed upon them avidly, but it is essential at this time if success is to be assured to have an artificial in one's box that is a reasonable likeness. This pattern is usually fished on the surface as a dry fly, and should be cast out in the vicinity of rising trout and left to lie still; sometimes an occasional tweak on the line to provide animation is necessary to attract attention to your offering. I prefer not to grease the cast, or to oil the fly, for there are times when the trout will completely ignore this pattern when fished dry, but will accept it eagerly as it begins to sink. At times the trout will also take it if it is retrieved slowly just under the surface, but why this should be I am unable to comprehend as this is quite contrary to the action or behaviour of the natural.

A relatively easy pattern to tie, except possibly for the legs. Take the brown tying silk down to the bend and tie in three strands of black dyed condor or peacock herl; these are then twisted anti-clockwise and wound two-thirds of the way up the shank and tied in. Then take two strands of the same material and tie these in by the butts, one each side of the body sloping back and under the body to form the long trailing legs. Two natural black cock hackles should then be wound on with the convex sides against each other. Finally wind on a single strand of black herl in front of the hackle and behind the eye to form the head.

Dressing

Hook	U/E size 12
Silk	Brown Pearsall's gossamer
Body	Three strands of black dyed condor or peacock herl
Hackle	Two natural black cock wound on so that the convex sides are turned against each other
Head	Single strand of black dyed condor or peacock
Legs	Two strands of black dyed condor or peacock tied with points trailing back

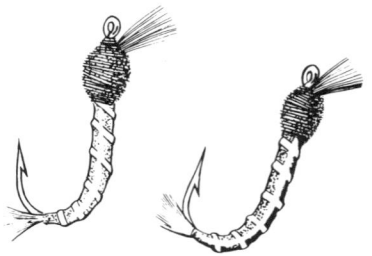

32 Hatching Midge Pupa

One of the earliest patterns I evolved specifically for fishing in still water, this is meant to represent the pupae of the chironomidae (midges) hanging in the surface film preparatory to hatching into the adult winged midge (buzzer). Unlike Geoffrey Bucknall's pattern, the Footballer, which is intended to represent the ascending pupa, and is consequently fished with a certain amount of movement, my pattern is intended to be fished with little or no movement in the surface film. It was therefore essential to have a pattern that was a good likeness of the natural and as the only ones available at the time were but poor representations, it was this aspect that I concentrated on. Working from enlarged photographs of the natural, I eventually evolved a pattern which appeared most lifelike, and has since accounted for large numbers of trout. They are dressed in various colours to match the naturals and I usually tie them on straight eyed hooks, which enables me to mount two or three direct onto the leader at three foot intervals

54

and stopped with blood knots. Mounted in this manner with the leader lightly greased they will float head upright in the surface film, where the trout expect to find the naturals. I usually mount a large well greased sedge on the point with two or three pupae at intervals along the leader, and these are then cast out to rising trout during a buzzer rise, normally in calm conditions very early in the morning or late in the evening. I allow them to lie without movement where the trout will often accept them confidently. The take is often very gentle, however, so the line should be watched carefully at all times. They may also be mounted on the point and on droppers in the traditional manner, but then I find they are more effective if retrieved very slowly, or at times even medium fast.

In the early part of the evening before the general rise commences, many trout will be cruising near the bottom waiting to feed on the ascending pupae, and during this period I have taken many fish, as follows. Replace the artificial pupa on the top dropper with a large well oiled sedge pattern, and then thoroughly degrease the two or three remaining pupae on the leader, cast out and allow them to sink until they are hanging below the sedge which will then act like a tiny float. This is particularly effective in a good ripple as the sedge floating on the surface imparts a most enticing movement to the pupa below.

This is quite a tricky pattern to dress as it is important to get the various materials used in the right proportions to give a lifelike silhouette. Commence by taking your tying silk two thirds of the way round the bend of the hook, then tie in several strands of white nylon filaments to project about $\frac{1}{8}$ inch below to form the tail (tracheal gills). The strip of PVC is then tied in and left hanging, followed by a length of silver lurex for ribbing the body. This is followed with a length of marabou silk of the chosen colour, which may if desired have a strand or two of firebrand fluorescent wool mixed in. Wind two thirds of the way up the shank and tie in. Next rib the body with the silver lurex and wind the strip of PVC over the top to cover the body completely. Two or three strands of peacock herl or brown dyed turkey are then wound on to form the thorax, but before this is built up to the required thickness a short length of white fluorescent wool is trapped under the strands pointing forward over the eye of the hook to represent the breathing filaments. This can then be trimmed to the right length after the thorax is completed and tied in.

Dressing

Hook	Straight eye round bend size 10 to 14
Silk	As body colour
Body	Black, brown, red or green marabou silk with a strand or two of fluorescent firebrand wool of the same colour mixed in if desired
Tag	Strand of white nylon filaments projecting below bend by ⅛ inch
Rib	Silver lurex
Body Covering	A ⅛ inch wide strip of natural colour PVC (the new latex material may be used)
Thorax	Three strands of peacock herl or brown dyed turkey
Head Filaments	Short strand of white fluorescent wool

33 The Lake Olive

There are many species of upwinged flies indigenous to most lakes and reservoirs, and although generally speaking they are more important to both fish and fisherman on the rocky lakes and tarns in Wales and Scotland, they are occasionally of importance on lowland stillwaters. The two most important species are the pond and lake olives, and as they are very similar one pattern will usually suffice to imitate both. Hatches of either species are usually confined to the middle of the day, and unfortunately are often on the sparse side, so seldom do they elicit a substantial surface rise from the trout, at least on most lowland waters. During these sparse rises a nymph, hatching nymph or wet fly fished just under the surface film is usually more effective, but should a good hatch occur it is then essential to have a lifelike dry pattern to offer them. Hatches of these upwinged flies seldom if ever occur in deep water, so when they are anticipated you will be well advised to seek them in water about six feet deep or less, in the vicinity of extensive weed beds. The artificial should be well treated with floatant and can either be cast quickly to rising fish or alternatively it may be cast out and left to lie still to await the attention of any cruising trout. While practically any of the host of dry olive river patterns may be used, I feel it is well worth while having a pattern in one's fly box that is specifically designed to represent these stillwater olives. For this reason I have chosen a pattern designed by the well known stillwater fly fisher C. F. Walker.

This is a fairly straightforward pattern to dress. Start by tying in a bunch of fibres of dark blue dun cock to form the tails, follow this with a length of silver tinsel for ribbing the body. The body material of three or four strands of pale grey brown condor herl is then wound on, followed by a bunch of fibres from a pale waterhen body feather to form the wings. Finally the leg hackle of pale brassy blue dun cock is then wound on and tied in.

Dressing

Hook	U/E size 10 to 14
Silk	Grey
Tail	Fibres from a dark blue dun cock's spade or saddle feather
Rib	Silver tinsel
Body	Three or four fibres of pale grey brown condor herl
Wings	A bunch of fibres from a pale water hen or coot feather
Hackle	Pale brassy-blue dun cock

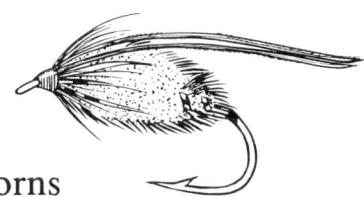

34 The Longhorns

This is another relatively new specialized still water pattern which was first introduced by Richard Walker in the early 1970s and like many of his designs is a very killing pattern when fished in the correct manner. However, I feel I must point out that whilst he refers to it as a pattern to represent the pupae of many species of sedge flies, this is a little misleading, for with its long trailing antennae and bushy hackle it bears them little resemblance. It does though bear a striking similarity to many species of sedge pupae in the act of hatching into the adult, which in many cases takes place on or in the surface film. I feel it would therefore be much more accurate to refer to this pattern as representing a hatching sedge pupa. Richard states that he allows it to sink two to three feet before retrieving steadily, and that this method has caught him a great many trout. I can't help thinking that he would have probably caught an even greater number if he had fished this a little nearer the surface, as this is where most trout will be seeking and expecting to find the hatching pupa. This artificial should be fished on the point either with a floating line and a de-greased leader, or with a slow sinking line. It is equally effective fished from a boat or bank from late June to early September. This pattern is dressed in three basic colour combinations which are adequate to cover the somewhat restricted colour range of the naturals.

The dressing procedure is as follows. Take the tying silk down to the bend and there tie in a length of fine gold wire with which to rib the body, then tie in two long strands of sea green dyed ostrich herl to form the body. These should be twisted together in an anti-clockwise direction, wound up the shank to the eye in a clockwise direction, and then wound back to the bend over itself and back once again to the eye where it is tied in. The resulting thickly formed body should be ribbed with the gold wire, wound on in an anti-clockwise direction. The thorax, composed of one strand of sepia ostrich herl, is then tied in at the eye and wound down over the ribbed body for a third of the length of the hook shank, then wound back to the eye and tied in. Next tie in at the eye and sloping back over the body for twice its length two dark strands of pheasant tail fibre. Finally, providing you have left sufficient room imme-diately behind the eye, the partridge hackle is wound on and tied in with a whip finish.

Dressing

Hook	D/E size 10 or 12
Silk	Dark brown
Rib	Fine gold wire
Body	Two strands of ostrich herl dyed sea green
Thorax	One strand of ostrich herl dyed sepia brown
Antennae	Two strands of dark pheasant-tail fibre
Hackle	Brown partridge hackle

The other two colour combinations are (1) light chestnut thorax and sea green body tied with light brown silk; (2) light chestnut thorax and amber body tied with bright vermilion silk.

---

35 The Ombudsman

This is a new pattern developed specially for stillwater fishing by Brian Clarke who is best known for his most excellent book *The Pursuit of Stillwater Trout*. While Brian admits this was originally intended as a general attractor pattern, it has during the past three seasons proved to be an excellent early season fly, particularly when fished slowly and deep. If one examines this artificial closely it does bear more than a passing resemblance in shape, colour and even size to a mature alder larva, and this would probably account for its success when fished in the manner described, as it is during the early part of the season that trout feed on the natural alder larvae which are of course found on or near the bottom. I understand that this artificial has also accounted for fair numbers of trout later in the season when fished nearer the surface, so I think that Brian's original intention to provide a general attractor can also be justified as it could be argued that it also resembles many of the darker species of sedge pupae. However I have included it in this section to be fished as an imitation of the alder larva, and to obtain the best results it should be fished on the point in conjunction with a sinking line, and then retrieved along the bottom as slowly as possible with frequent pauses.

Rather a tricky pattern to dress as it is important to tie in the materials in the right proportions. One third along the hook shank tie in brown silk and wind down to the bend. There tie in nine or ten inches of fine copper wire, followed by three strands of peacock herl, which is then wound back up to end of thread where they are tied off. Rib the body with the fine copper wire, and then build this up in front of the body into a cylindrical flat-topped section, which provides both weight and a base on which to tie in the rolled mottled turkey tail feather fibres. These should be tied in close along the top of the body projecting well beyond the

59

bend. A light red cock hackle is then tied in sloping well back, and the final operation is to build up a bold head in front of this with the tying silk.

Dressing

Hook	D/E size 8 to 12 longish shank wide gape
Silk	Brown
Body	Three strands bronze/green peacock herl taken from close to the eye
Rib	Fine copper wire
Wings	Sections taken from speckled brown turkey or cock pheasant wing quills and rolled along and over the body and projecting well beyond bend where the ends should be brought together almost to a point
Hackle	Pale red cock tied in sloping well back

36 The Pheasant Tail Nymph

This well known pattern was designed over a quarter of a century ago by that great and distinguished river keeper Frank Sawyer. Originally developed for upstream nymph fishing in rivers, it has in more recent years proved to be equally acceptable on many still waters, and is now considered an excellent general pattern to imitate most of the darker nymphs of upwinged flies to be found on both lakes and reservoirs. This is a weighted pattern and was designed to be fished well under the surface to represent the immature nymphs. Over the years Sawyer developed a technique of fishing this weighted type of nymph which he referred to as the 'induced take method', fully described in that marvellous book *Nymph Fishing in Theory and Practice* by the late Major Oliver Kite who so ably assisted Sawyer to publicize the method. This technique like the nymph was intended purely for fishing rivers but when one considers it logically it is really but a variation of the equally successful sink and draw method which is so popular on still water today. Therefore, it would seem this is the best way to fish this pattern in still water, and is indeed the method I have always adopted. I normally use a light rod, a floating line and mount this nymph alone on the point of a long leader.

60

I often find it effective during the middle hours of the day, particularly when bank fishing. When space permits I like to work my way along the bank casting as I go and retrieving slowly in this sink and draw style. The copper wire used to weight this nymph also replaces the normal tying silk, and as this was a completely new idea, Sawyer is quite rightly credited with its invention.

An exceptionally simple and quick pattern to dress, it is another good fly for the beginner to start on. Commence by winding the fine copper wire around the hook shank immediately behind the eye taking it about a third of the way down the shank. It is then wound back and forth over this area building up a considerable hump, both to provide weight and to simulate the thorax of the natural nymph. After the thorax has been formed the wire is then wound down the shank to the bend, where three or four long reddish fibres from the centre of a cock pheasant tail are tied in with the wire. These fibres are tied in with the points protruding by about $\frac{1}{8}$ in. to represent the tails of the natural nymph. The wire is then wound back to the eye to be followed by the pheasant tail fibres which should completely cover the copper wire. These fibres are then tied in at the eye with the wire, and then the darker butts taken over the top of the thorax where they are doubled and re-doubled to form the wing cases before being finally secured at the eye again with the wire.

Dressing

Hook	D/E size 10 to 16
Body	Formed with fine reddish copper wire and covered with three or four long fibres of reddish cock pheasant centre tail
Tail	Formed from the tips of the cock pheasant fibres used for the body
Wing Cases	Formed from the darker butts of the cock pheasant body fibres

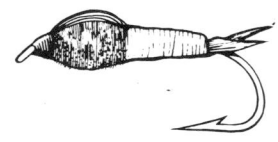

37 The PVC Nymph

One of my oldest patterns, I originally developed it as a copy of many of the olive nymphs found in rivers, but in recent years I have found it is equally effective on still water to represent nymphs of the pond or lake olives. At the time I first evolved this pattern, Sawyer's pheasant tail nymph was rapidly increasing in popularity, and while I found this an excellent artificial to represent many of the darker species of nymphs, particularly when fished with the induced take method, I felt it was the wrong colour for most of the olive nymphs, nor was it a particularly close representation. The new pattern which was based on Sawyer's use of copper wire immediately proved to be a resounding success, and since those early days has steadily increased in popularity, accounting for many large trout both in rivers and still water. These days when fishing I always carry the two patterns, as they are complementary. On still water I usually fish the PVC nymph by the sink and draw method, on a long leader of at least 18ft. Where weed beds are present, trout often move along the edges looking for emergent nymphs, so at this time a most effective and rewarding method is to cast over the weed and let your nymph sink several feet down the edge before retrieving it. Be alert for takes on the sink as well as on the draw.

This is not a particularly easy pattern to dress, as it takes a little practice to get the proportions of the materials correct. Take a length of copper wire and build up a substantial thorax a little way behind the eye and then continue with a single winding down to the bend and cut off surplus. Brown tying silk should then be wound on at the bend, where a strip of PVC $\frac{1}{8}$ in. wide is secured. This is followed with three strands of olive or olive brown condor herl, or substitute, tied with the fine tops protruding about $\frac{1}{8}$ in. to form the tails. The silk is then wound up to the eye followed by the three strands of condor which are wound evenly over the copper wire up to eye where they are secured. The silk is wound back behind the thorax and the PVC strip is then wound over the condor, up to the thorax and tied in. The silk is then taken back to the eye where the wing cases of two or three dark pheasant tail fibres are doubled and redoubled over the top of the thorax and secured.

Dressing

Hook	D/E size 12 to 17
Silk	Brown
Tails	Formed from the tips of the three strands of olive condor herl used for the body
Underbody and Thorax	Copper wire
Overbody and Thorax	Three strands of olive or olive brown condor herl or substitute
Body Covering	A ⅛ in. wide strip of PVC wound and overlapped up to thorax
Wing Pads	Three strands of dark pheasant tail herl

N.B. A cut strip of latex may be used in place of the PVC. Personally I prefer PVC as it has less stretch, so is easier to cut and handle. More important it is less opaque, so the body colour shows through better.

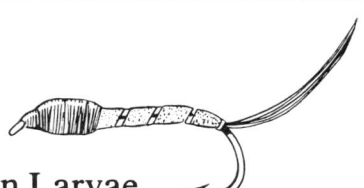

38 Red or Green Larvae

A pattern I developed several years ago to represent the larvae of various species of chironimids (midges), these imitations have since accounted for many trout, particularly in the early part of the season. At this time of the year the natural larvae are most prolific and form a major part of the trout's diet. They vary in size from half an inch to well over an inch in length and the predominant colours are red, brown, green or varying shades in between. The red are probably the best known and they are commonly referred to as bloodworms. The trout browse on them when they leave their retreats in the mud, detritus or weed near the bottom to feed. Unfortunately at this stage they are extremely difficult to imitate as they move or swim with a peculiar undulating or figure of eight lashing movement. This particular artificial has enjoyed a certain amount of success due no doubt to the long curly fibres used for the tail which do provide some degree of animation. It may be fished from either bank or anchored boat, utilizing a slow sink line in shallow water or a fast sink in deep water. This artificial should always be fished on the point, and retrieved very slowly along the bottom, giving the line frequent twitches.

A fairly simple and straightforward pattern to tie, it should prove popular with most amateur fly dressers. The tying silk, preferably brown, should be wound along the shank to the bend where the long tail, formed from two or three strongly curved fibres of ibis or heron, is tied in. These are followed with a length of narrow silver lurex with which to rib the body. The body material, composed of three or four strands of condor herl or substitute mixed with a judicious amount of fluorescent floss of the same colour, is then wound three-quarters of the way up the shank, ribbed with the lurex and tied off. The thorax of buff coloured condor or pale brown dyed turkey feather fibres should then be tied in immediately behind the eye.

Dressing

Hook	D/E size 8 to 12 long shank
Silk	Brown
Tail	Two or three very curly fibres from an ibis quill (red) or dyed heron red or green to match body colour
Body	Three or four crimson or olive dyed condor herls or substitute mixed with a strand of fluorescent silk floss of the same colour
Thorax	Two or three fibres of buff condor or pale brown dyed turkey

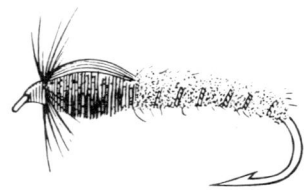

39 Sedge Pupa

Without doubt this has proved to be one of my most successful stillwater patterns, and during the past few years seems to have accounted for a great many trout in various parts of the country. During the late 50s and early 60s I fished Blagdon and Chew Valley lakes fairly regularly and I soon came to realize that many species of sedge flies were prolific on these waters. While I enjoyed a certain amount of success with the floating artificial sedge at the time, I felt sure that an artificial to represent the pupal stage should prove more effective as these were constantly to be found in the stomach contents of trout. At the time no such artificials were available, so I eventually decided to dress a pattern myself from the various colour photographs I had obtained of the naturals over quite a long period. Probably more by luck than judgement my initial pattern met with immediate success, so over the intervening years apart from a few minor alterations it has changed but little. I dress these in four basic colours, orange, green, brown and cream, as this more than adequately covers the colour range of the natural pupae. Many species of sedge flies hatch in open water or via emergent vegetation along the shoreline, therefore the pupae have to swim either to the surface or to the shore and at this stage they are both attractive to and vulnerable to the depredations of the trout. The artificial sedge pupa may be fished in two ways, either at midwater or near the bottom on a fast sink line or just under the surface on a slow sink or floating line. It should always be fished on the point and retrieved at a medium pace with occasional pauses. This is a pattern which can be used with confidence from late June onwards, and while it seems to be most effective during late afternoon or early evenings it will take fish at any time of the day. I do have slight preference for the green-bodied pattern during late June and early July and the cream in September, but the colour to be used will depend on the species of sedge fly hatching at the time. When boat fishing, particularly during July, I love to drift in a good breeze with one of these pupae patterns on the point, and an Invicta or Longhorn on the middle dropper with a well greased dry sedge on the top dropper to act as an attractor.

This is a fairly simple and straightforward pattern to dress, so even the learner may be encouraged to attempt it. First wind the brown tying silk down the shank to the bend, and then tie in a length of narrow silver lurex. Next wind on the body material of the appropriate coloured seal's fur two thirds up the shank, rib with the lurex and tie off. This is followed with two or three fibres of dark brown dyed condor herl or turkey to form the thorax, and then two or three fibres of pale brown condor or heron herl are doubled and redoubled over the top to form the wing cases, which are then tied off behind the eye. Finally tie in a rusty hen hackle sloping well back, one and a half to two turns.

Dressing

Hook	D/E size 10 to 12 long shank, wide gape
Tying Silk	Brown
Body	Cream, brown, orange or green seal's fur; a little fluorescent floss silk may be wound sparsely over the last two colours
Rib	Narrow silver lurex or oval tinsel
Thorax	Dark brown condor herl or dyed turkey (light brown with brown-bodied pattern)
Wing Cases	Two or three pale coloured feather fibres doubled and redoubled (dark brown for brown bodied pattern)
Hackle	Rusty hen hackle tied sparsely $1\frac{1}{2}$ to 2 turns

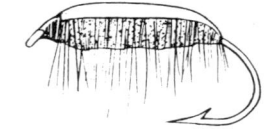

40 The Shrimper

As the name implies this is a pattern to represent the fresh-water shrimp, which I originally developed for river fishing. It has since proved to be equally effective in still water where the natural is sometimes found in even greater numbers. There are several different patterns available today, but I have decided to describe my own, as on balance I still feel the colour and shape is closer to the natural, although in very weedy water Richard Walker's pattern dressed with weight on top of the shank to make it fish upside down has a lot to commend it. The naturals in lakes are usually found in areas of shallower weedy water, and during the winter months when other forms of food are in short supply they form a major part of the trout's diet. Unfortunately by the time the season opens the majority of trout have transferred their attention to other more varied types of food and will only occasionally deign to look at a natural shrimp. Even so for some strange reason artificial patterns do account for considerable numbers of trout during an average season, so it is a useful artificial for the angler to carry in his fly box. This is yet another fly that should be fished on the point, and retrieved along the lake bed as slowly as possible with frequent pauses. As it is a heavily weighted pattern and is best fished in shallow water (up to 6ft in depth) it can be presented quite successfully on a floating line utilizing a long leader; alternatively, a slow sink or sink tip line with a leader of standard length may be used. Personally I prefer the former as fished on a floating line it does tend to impart a slight sink and draw action to the artificial which seems to prove more attractive to the fish.

This is a very satisfying pattern to dress as it has a most lifelike appearance when completed. Take some fine copper wire and wind onto the hook shank thickening in centre to form a considerable hump. Then wind on orange silk at the bend tying in a strip cut from PVC or the new latex rubber sheet—this should be about $\frac{3}{16}$ in. wide in the middle tapering at each end. This is followed with an olive or honey coloured hackle tied in by the tip. The body material of olive brown seal's fur or marabou silk is then tied in and wound over the copper wire up to the eye, followed by the hackle which is wound along the body palmer fashion. This hackle should then be trimmed along the top, and finally the PVC or latex is stretched over the top of the body and tied off at the eye.

N.B. To represent the mating colour of the shrimp during June and July, a small amount of orange fluorescent silk may be wound over the body material.

Dressing

Hook	D/E size 10 to 14 Limerick
Silk	Orange
Body	Fine copper wire wound in thickly at centre to form hump, covered with olive brown seal's fur
Hackle	Honey dun or olive cock
Back	Strip of PVC or latex rubber. Length of hook. Cut wide in centre and tapering each end. The PVC is probably to be preferred, since it stretches less, is easier to handle, and is less opaque than latex.

41 Small Hatching Midge

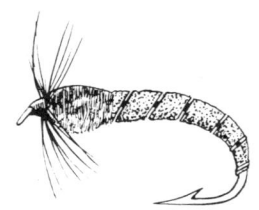

I first developed this pattern for fishing at Hanningfield reservoir in the late 1960s, when tremendous hatches of small chironomids became a feature of the fishing during the afternoons from late June until well into August. Once an emergence of these tiny creatures commenced the trout became preoccupied feeding on them and were difficult to take on normal patterns. This situation also applies on many other still waters, although often to a lesser degree. The new pattern proved to be very successful, but I quickly discovered that to obtain the best results it was necessary to use a different technique for presenting it. The best hatches seem to occur on relatively calm days, when given a fair breeze with a nice ripple the trout invariably feed in a straight line upwind, rising regularly every few feet. As most of these small midges tend to hatch out in deepish water, the best opportunities are provided from a boat, and under these conditions it is best to anchor in a wind lane and cast to rising fish when they come in range. On the other hand in a flat calm the trout usually rise in a circular or zigzag movement, and it is then best to allow the boat to drift up on them. They are very wary and easily put down when so engaged, and I have found from bitter experience that absolute silence and minimum movement is essential if any success at all is to be expected. I always lightly oil this pattern as I have found it is most successful when fished in the surface film. It should be mounted alone on the point on as long a leader as you can manage. My preference is 18 to 20 feet and I use it in conjunction with as light a floating line as the rod can take. Quick and accurate casting is essential as the fly must be presented immediately in front of the last rise, and if your judgement has been good you can expect a take almost as soon as the fly alights on the water. I dress this artificial in four colours, red, brown, green or black, but I hasten to add that the black midge is more likely to be observed in the mornings or late evenings during the spring or autumn.

As this pattern is dressed on rather small hooks it is a

little tricky to tie. Start by winding the tying silk down the shank and slightly round the bend. Tie in a length of narrow silver lurex and take two close turns and secure, then tie in two strands of condor herl or substitute of the chosen colour and wind two thirds of way up the shank. Next wind the rib of silver lurex over the body and tie in. Take one or two strands of brown dyed turkey herl, form the thorax and secure behind the eye. Finally wind on the hackle of small honey cock one and a half to two turns.

Dressing

Hook	D/E size 14 or 16
Silk	Brown gossamer
Body	Two turns of silver lurex, followed by two strands of condor herl, dark red, green, orange, brown or black. A small amount of fluorescent silk of same colour may be mixed with body material if desired
Rib	Narrow silver lurex
Thorax	One or two strands of dark brown turkey herl
Hackle	Small honey cock tied sparsely

42 The Snail (Floating)

This is a most unusual pattern and I am quite sure that the vast majority of anglers do not carry an artificial that resembles the natural at all, except possibly a black and peacock spider which if greased to float is a reasonable substitute. Even so this in no way compares with this fine imitative pattern perfected by that superb amateur fly dresser Cliff Henry many years ago. First of all let me point out that this is not an artificial that you will use very often, but on those rare occasions when it is required it is worth its weight in gold. If during a hot calm day or evening in July or August there should be a heavy rise of trout and they will not look at anything you or any other anglers present are offering, then it is an odds on they are taking floating snail. The fish take them down in a very leisurely fashion, with a slow head and tail rise, and it is practically impossible to tell the difference between this rise and that to the much more common buzzer. It is also similar to the rise of trout to caenis or small midges, so therein lies one of the main difficulties. Several times I have literally missed the boat, because I have not realized until too late that they were on the snail, as at this time they usually become very selective and will ignore all other types of food. To complicate matters further the snail floats pad uppermost just below or in the surface film and they are quite impossible to see unless you look directly down into the water. There are apparently several species of snail that rise to the surface in this manner including the common wandering snail, and they vary in size from as large as a pea down to as small as a lead shot. At certain times of the year usually in hot calm weather they rise and float in the surface, sometimes only for hours but more often for several days. I remember one season at Hanningfield reservoir where this phenomenon occurred in one particular corner every day for many weeks, but I am sure this was most unusual as I have never heard of it being repeated there or elsewhere. The fishing technique is very simple but effective. Tie your floating snail on the point on a floating line, cast it out in the vicinity of rising fish and wait for a trout to take, no movement is required but the line should be carefully observed for the draw as the trout accepts.

This is an extremely simple pattern to dress, but the preparation is a little tedious. The first operation is to make the body. This is formed from a piece of cork or alternatively the more modern plastazote may be used as a substitute. Trim to a pear shape, but with a flat top to simulate the pad of the snail. This should be cut a little shorter than the shank of the hook being used. It is then split along the centre half way through and glued onto the shank of the hook, with the pad close to the eye of the hook. When it is thoroughly dry and secure, the cork body may be covered with two strands of stripped peacock quill. The bronze-green herl should be used, stripping two thirds of each strand, and then tying in by the stripped ends just above the bend. They are then wound closely up the pear shaped body, and tied off round the top at the widest part. If the herl has been stripped correctly it will be found when wound on, that the last two or three turns near the pad form a rim of unstripped herl. The completed body may then be well varnished to give longer life.

Dressing

Hook	D/E size 10 to 14, wide gape
Silk	Black
Body	A pear shaped section of cork glued around hook shank
Body Covering	Partly stripped bronze-green peacock quill

43 The Tadpolly

This is a pattern that I developed comparatively recently to represent the common tadpole as I was unable to find a trace of any existing patterns at the time. Since then I have discovered the existence of one other artificial called the 'Tadpole Streamer', perfected by Taff Price and listed in his recent and excellent book *Lures for Game, Sea or Coarse Fishing*. It is very similar indeed to my own pattern with one major difference. Taff suggests clipped deer hair for the body, and while this looks fine it takes a long time to dress. I am amazed no one has suggested an artificial to represent the tadpole before as they are very common in many ponds, lakes and even some reservoirs, and there is no doubt the trout will accept them readily enough when they come across them. I first tied this pattern a couple of years ago when trout fishing in South Africa, as I found partly digested tadpoles in so many of the trout I spooned out that I felt the need of an artificial to imitate them. The resulting pattern, although quite simple and straightforward, proved to be very effective, and I have subsequently taken considerable numbers of home trout on it. In fact so readily has it been accepted on many waters I am inclined to think that trout may feed on the natural far more often than is generally supposed, and this could well account for the success of the common and widely used black type of lure. The Tadpolly should always be fished on its own on the point, and I have found it is best retrieved at a medium speed either on a slow sink or fast sink line. It seems to be more effective during the spring or early summer when the naturals are most common, and I also favour fishing it in shallow rather than deep water.

A simple and quick pattern to dress, the Tadpolly is

made from common materials that should be found in any fly dresser's kit. Take three black cock hackles about the same length as the hook, and tie them in side by side to form the tail. Next spin some black seal's fur on the silk and wind up the shank to the eye fairly thickly. Finally tie in three or four green-bronze peacock herls a little behind the eye and then build them up to form the characteristic head/body of the natural tadpole, adding a dab or two of varnish between turns.

Dressing

Hook	D/E size 10 or 12
Silk	Black
Tail	Three black cock (or hen) hackles about same length as hook, tied in near the bend and projecting well beyond
Body	Black seal's fur
Head	Three or four green-bronze peacock herls

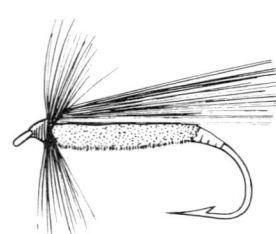

44 Walker's Sedge

As the name suggests this is another pattern from that ace of anglers Richard Walker. Any pattern designed by the maestro is obviously worthy of serious consideration and this pattern is no exception. In fact I think this is one of his most effective patterns, as it has provided me with quite a few trout in the past four or five years. While it looks like many other artificial sedges, appearances can often be deceptive, and this is a point in case, as it has been dressed for a particular way of fishing. The head hackles are long and stiff, the wings are of cock hackle that tends to repel water, and even the body material of ostrich herl is very buoyant.

The fishing technique with this pattern is to waterproof the fly with a good silicone and, having cast it out, to draw it fast across the surface, fast enough so that it rises up on its hackle tips, with the wing, body and hook cocked up clear of the water. This produces a wake very similar to that made by some species of natural sedges. Sometimes the fly will be taken on the move, at other times as it stops between retrieves.

I look upon this pattern as representing the darker species of sedge flies and as being complementary to my own G & H Sedge, which is intended to imitate many of the lighter species, as they are both excellent floaters. In the section describing my own patterns I suggested many different ways in which they can be fished, but Walker's pattern lends itself particularly to fast fishing. In fact it cannot be fished too fast at times, and Walker himself suggests to achieve the necessary speed one should lower the rod parallel to the water, and lift it vertically at the same time as the retrieve is made. This will cause it to skate over the surface, which will often prove irresistible to the trout.

As previously explained the choice of materials is particularly important in the dressing of this pattern. Whip the tying silk closely down the shank to the bend and varnish. While the varnish is still tacky, wind on at the bend a small tip of arc chrome D.F. wool, followed by the main body composed of three strands of chestnut ostrich herl and tie off a little short of the eye. This should then be clipped as closely as possible to give a velvet appearance to the body. The wing is then tied on sloping back over the body, and this is composed of a bunch of natural red cock hackle fibres clipped square and level with the hook bend. Finally tie in behind the eye two long-fibred, top quality, stiff, natural red cock hackles.

Dressing

Hook	D/E size 8 to 10 long shank, round bend
Silk	Brown
Tip	Arc chrome D.F. wool
Body	Three strands of chestnut ostrich herl
Wing	Bunch of natural red cock hackles tied sloping back and clipped square at bend
Hackle	Two stiff natural red cock hackles

Lures

After considerable thought I have decided to deal with the flies in this section in a slightly different manner. In the previous two sections I have included details of the fishing technique individually with each pattern, but as the basic methods for fishing lures are similar for most patterns, I will discuss the general techniques separately.

Lures are basically attractor patterns and are invariably dressed on long shank, tandem or even treble hooks and vary in length from an inch to well over three inches. Since its inception lure fishing has been looked down upon by the traditionalists, for unfortunately in the early days the practitioners of this style of fishing were quite content to spend all day fishing from the bank in one spot, mechanically casting out the same lure as far as possible and then stripping it back as fast as possible. Undoubtedly trout can be caught by this method through sheer persistence, and even today one will come across a certain percentage of anglers on every still water, still content to practise it and progress no further. This is a great pity as lure fishing like any other style requires specialized techniques to obtain the best results. Anyone doubting this statement, should make the effort to watch one of the experts at work. Anglers of the calibre of Bob Church and Dick Shrive who tend to specialize in lure fishing produce an artistry in this form of trout fishing which is almost unbelievable, and under reasonable conditions can produce trout after trout as if by magic.

The real artistry in lure fishing lies in the retrieve, and the manipulation of the fly line in the angler's hands. I can assure you that most of the really successful stillwater anglers, whether they are fishing with lures or imitation patterns, have a certain indefinable rhythm with the hands when retrieving, which marks them out as a class apart. Some more fortunate than others seem to be born with this attribute, while others only achieve it after many years of experience. Many of us never attain it, and alas will never be more than reasonably successful fishermen. However, the other aspects which provide in most cases satisfactory bags of trout on most waters are largely a question of commonsense and I can do no better than to quote Bob Church who once said 'It is only necessary to work on the principle

74

of popular patterns and prevailing conditions equal the need for a certain type of fly line and speed to retrieve for that particular day'.

Today the lure fisherman is well catered for with fly lines. There are many types available, floating, slow sink, fast sink, Hi D (very fast sink) or sink tip, and in addition there are even lead cored lines which are usually used for deep water fishing or trolling, although I do not really approve of the latter. At first glance the tyro may be confused by this choice, but again it is really a question of commonsense. As a general rule floating lines are used for fishing shallow water or near the surface or for nymph fishing. Slow sink lines are used for retrieving fast just under the surface, for fishing near the bottom in shallow or weedy water or for very slow retrieving in deep water and they are also very useful for fishing the sink and draw method in deep water. Fast sink lines are invariably used for retrieving lures medium to fast in deep water, and Hi D lines used for fast retrieves near the bottom in very deep water.

The next step is to consider when to use these different types of lines, and this will depend on several factors, the weather, period of the year and behaviour of the trout. The following examples or basic rules will I hope assist the inexperienced lure angler in his choice of line and method of fishing on any given day, depending whether he is fishing from boat or bank.

Early in the season when water temperatures are still fairly low it is usually best to concentrate on the deeper water, fishing along or near the bottom, with sinking lines, either from the bank or an anchored boat. In summer when the temperature is higher on bright calm days it is best to concentrate on water of medium depth during the day, using sink tip or slow sink lines from the bank or sink tip or fast sink from a boat. Floating or slow sink lines should be used at this time in shallow water early morning or late evening. In very hot bright weather though it may be better to fish deeper water during the day. When trout are rising or showing occasionally near the surface, always use a floating or slow sink line, bearing in mind that the latter is usually better in calm conditions. During fairly windy dull weather fishing is usually more rewarding as the trout, particularly rainbows, will be near the surface even if they are not actually showing. Under these conditions the water will often be coloured so the retrieve needs to be quite slow, and the fly will often be accepted on the drop. From the bank a floating or sink tip line should be used, while from a boat a sink tip or slow sink. In warm weather when the temperature is high, should the water be clear with a good ripple a lure retrieved fairly fast just under the surface from boat or bank can be very killing.

The choice of lure or colour can sometimes be very important, but this can only be appreciated with experience. As a general rule, however, you won't go far wrong if you observe the following. White or pale coloured lures are best fished near the surface, while black or dark patterns should be favoured for fishing near the bottom except in very bright weather when the reverse often applies. Black lures seem to take more trout early in the year, and patterns with orange in them always seem to be more effective in the latter half of the season. In addition it should also be pointed out that lures that are streamlined with little dressing are seldom effective when retrieved slowly. Lures should invariably be fished on the point, and while many authorities consider they should always be fished on their own, there is in my opinion no reason why other patterns should not be fished on the droppers, providing of course they complement the lure being used or the speed of retrieve.

In the early days most lure fishers preferred the bank, but in recent years boat fishing has become very popular as it offers a greater scope. Not only can lures be fished from an anchored boat just as effectively as from the bank, but we now have sophisticated devices such as controllers and lee boards to assist us in presentation.

45 The Ace of Spades

Typical of the new breed of lures that has appeared during the last decade, this pattern has enjoyed considerable success since it was first introduced by that celebrated professional fly dresser David Collyer in the early 1970s. The wing is tied in the matuka style, which originated in New Zealand and proved to be so effective on artificials dressed to take the monster trout inhabiting the famous Lake Taupo in that country. It is a predominantly black pattern and is now being used by many anglers in preference to the common black lure, since general opinion seems to confirm that it is definitely superior. Like most dark coloured lures it seems to fish better in the early part of the season. At this time it is best retrieved deep, and to make the most of the matuka dressing it should be fished with frequent pauses to animate this wing to its best advantage.

A difficult pattern to dress neatly, this is definitely a pattern for the more experienced fly tyer. Take the black tying silk down the shank to the bend and secure a length of oval silver tinsel with which to rib the body. Next wind on a fairly thick body of black chenille nearly back to the eye. Then lay a black hen hackle vertically along the top of the body and tie in the butt end at the eye (this hackle should be a little over a third as long again as the hook used). The length of ribbing is then wound evenly back up the body over and through the hen hackle to the eye. The overwing of dark bronze mallard should then be secured on top of the eye, and sloping back over top of the main wing. The final operation is to tie in a few guinea fowl fibres under the eye sloping well back under the body.

Dressing

Hook	D/E size 6 to 12 long shank
Silk	Black
Rib	Oval silver tinsel
Body	Black chenille
Wing	Black hen tied matuka style as a crest
Overwing	Dark bronze mallard
Hackle	Guinea fowl

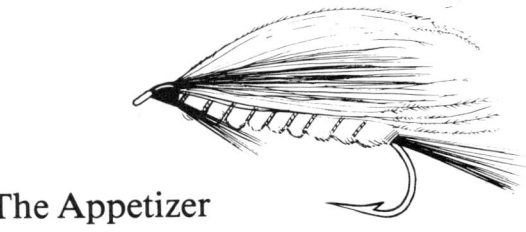

46 The Appetizer

This is one of the more recent creations of that fine still-water angler Bob Church, and follows a series of successful patterns that commenced in the mid 1960s. As Bob tends to specialize in lure fishing most of his better-known patterns are lures or attractors and this new pattern is no exception. First introduced in 1973, it was designed specifically to tempt the larger trout when they were feeding on fry during the latter half of the season. It has since proved its capabilities in this respect on many occasions, and has accounted for several limit catches of big trout including a magnificent bag limit of trout for Bob himself attaining a total weight of over 31lb. Like many of the paler coloured artificials this seems to produce the best results when fished near the surface. Bob confirms this as he suggests it is best fished on either a sink tip or slow sink line. It should be retrieved at a medium pace, with frequent pauses, as this works the very fine textured marabou herl to its best advantage.

To dress this pattern wind black tying silk down the hook shank to the bend and tie in a slightly thicker than normal tail of mixed fibres from orange, green and silver mallard feathers. Secure a length of silver tinsel to be used later for ribbing. The body of white chenille is then wound thickly along the shank to the eye, ribbed with the tinsel and tied off. The wing, composed of a generous spray of white marabou herl, should then be tied in sloping well back over the body extending well beyond the bend of the hook. An overwing is then formed from a spray of natural grey squirrel and tied in over the top. Finally tie in a throat hackle under the eye sloping well back, using the same mixture of feather fibres as used for the tail.

Dressing

Hook	D/E size 6 or 8 long shank
Silk	Black
Tail	Orange, green and silver mallard fibres mixed
Rib	Silver tinsel
Body	White chenille
Wing	White marabou herl—large spray
Overwing	Natural grey squirrel tail
Throat Hackle	Same mixture of fibres as used in tail

47 Aylott's Orange

I had great difficulty in deciding in which section to place this pattern as it is more suggestive than lure-like. Mainly because of its very bright body colouration, however, I decided it probably belonged to this group. Designed in the late 1970s by Richard Aylott it is undoubtedly his most successful pattern. It is now a well known and popular artificial on many reservoirs in the southern part of the country and has accounted for many large trout both brown and rainbow. Whether or not Richard originally designed this for a specific style of fishing I am not sure, but there is no doubt it is most successful fished slowly in the sink and draw style in conjunction with a floating line. As it seems to be more effective in the latter half of the season, I would imagine it is taken by the trout for an emerging sedge pupa. I have personally found it to be a useful pattern when the water is coloured with suspended mud on rough days, or a heavy algae bloom in hot weather. Under these conditions the bright fluorescent body is visible to the fish from a greater distance, and seems to be far more effective than standard pupa patterns. The reverse however applies in very clear water.

A relatively simple pattern to dress, it is another excellent artificial for the beginner. Wind black tying silk down to the bend, and there tie in a length of arc chrome D.F. wool. This should then be wound thickly around the shank towards the eye about two thirds of the length, forming a fat, juicy looking body. Next take a light red cock hackle and tie this in sparsely immediately in front of the body. Finally form a bold head from two or three peacock herls and tie off. To prolong the life of the body of this pattern it may be ribbed with fine nylon or silver wire.

Dressing

Hook	D/E size 12 or 14
Silk	Black
Body	Arc chrome D.F. wool
Hackle	Light red cock tied sparsely
Head	Two or three strands of peacock herl

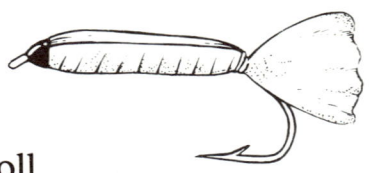

48 The Baby Doll

Here we have a pattern that will no doubt upset the purists, as anything less like a fly is hard to imagine. Let this not fool you, as it has proved to be one of the best lures to appear in recent years. It was originally devised in the early 1970s by Brian Kench for use at Ravensthorpe reservoir. Since then it has been popularized largely by Bob Church. Now well established nationwide as a top lure it has accounted for many large trout, both browns and rainbows, as well as many limit bags. This lure has also accounted for some very large specimen sized coarse fish, including bream over 10lb, carp over 20lb, tench over 5lb and many pike over 15lb. Why this lure should have proved to be so effective is difficult to substantiate, although white has always been a killing colour; the common white tandem lure has proved this point in the past. I am sure most experts will agree that this new pattern should now supersede the white lure. In practice it has been found to take trout on every type of still water and under all conditions. It seems to be killing fished at any depth, and as it is slightly buoyant can be retrieved slowly along the lake bed.

While this pattern is a quick lure to dress, the method of tying is a little unusual and may cause some problems initially. It is most important to use the right kind of brilliant white nylon wool, and 'Sirdar' brand baby wool was found to be the best, hence the lure's name. When tied with this wool, it stands out like a neon sign in the water. First of all well varnish the hook shank then cut off about nine inches of wool. This should be laid along the top of the shank as a large loop facing the eye, leaving an inch long single strand and a loop of similar length projecting for the tail. After securing both loops and short single strand with black tying silk, take the silk down to the eye of the hook. Next take the long single strand of baby wool left and loop this over the back of the long loop once. Then build up a long slim body and secure. Pull the long loop tightly along the back and tie in. Cut off any wool projecting over the eye, and then build up a large head with the silk. Finally cut the

short tail loop to about half an inch. Then with a needle
shred the three strands and cut into a bushy fish-tail shape.

49 The Black Bear's Hair Lure

Although this pattern is not so well known, and only has a
limited reputation in a few waters in Southern England I
have decided to include it, as it really is an exceptional lure.
Developed in the late 1960s by Cliff Henry, it has proved
to be one of his most successful artificials. On such reservoirs as Chew, Bough Beech and Hanningfield it has
accounted for many heavy limit bags of trout, and I have
personally found it particularly attractive to browns.
Dressed in the matuka fashion, the very soft bear's hair
gives it a very lively and attractive action. Both this pattern
and the Ace of Spades are in my opinion more effective
than the common black lure. Like all lures it is best fished
on the point, but unlike some lures it can often be fished
successfully with one or two other patterns on droppers. I
prefer to fish this pattern with either a floating or slow sink
line, and it should be retrieved in long slow or medium fast
retrieves with frequent pauses to activate the hair. In the
early part of the season it will take a lot of trout retrieved
slowly along or near the bottom, but later in the summer
it is particularly effective retrieved fairly fast just under the
surface.

The main ingredient required for dressing this pattern is
long soft bear hair on a thin soft supple skin. Having obtained this cut a strip about an inch wide and slightly
longer than the shank of the hook being used. From this
cut with a razor blade a strip about ⅛ in. wide. Tie in at the
bend of the hook a length of oval silver tinsel, then wind
black seal's fur fairly thickly along the shank to the eye.
Then take the ⅛ in. strip of bear's hair and lay it along the
top of the seal's fur so that a small section of the skin is
projecting beyond the bend, this is then secured matuka
fashion to the body with the tinsel and tied off at the eye.
The strip of skin projecting beyond the tail seems to give
this lure a slight but enticing wobble when retrieved.

Dressing

Hook	D/E size 8 or 10 long shank
Silk	Black
Rib	Oval silver tinsel
Body	Black seal's fur
Body Top	A $\frac{1}{8}$ in. wide strip of black bear hair with the skin cut a little longer than the hook shank

50 The Black and Orange Marabou

Here we have one of the new breed of stillwater flies, and this particular pattern has been designed by that fine amateur fly dresser Taff Price. This artificial incorporates a new material or perhaps it would be more correct to say fairly new to most fly dressers in this country. The name of the material is marabou which has been in general use in America for some time mainly in streamer type patterns, either replacing or being used in conjunction with hair. While it does not have the extreme durability of hair, I am sure its other qualities will endear it to the fly tyer. It is cheap and easily procured and most important of all it has a very lively action in the water, and for the lure fisherman it has the distinct advantage that it sinks rapidly once it is thoroughly wet. Without doubt more types of action can be imparted to this material than with most others as it is very fine and flexible and in the hands of a reasonably skilled angler it has proved to be irresistible to trout. Taff himself has had considerable success with this pattern, and it is now fast gaining converts especially in the southern part of the country on many of the new larger reservoirs. It seems to be most effective when retrieved along or near the bottom on a sinking or slow sinking line. To obtain the best results it should be worked all the time on the retrieve, to give the material the maximum animation.

While this is a straightforward pattern to dress, it does take a little time. Whip the shank well with black tying silk down to the bend and tie in a bunch of orange cock hackle fibres to form the tail. Next take a length of oval gold tinsel for ribbing and also tie this in at the bend, followed by a length of flat gold tinsel or lurex for the body. This should be wound tightly three quarters of the way up the shank, and then ribbed with the oval tinsel and tied in. We now tie in a substantial bunch of black marabou sloping back over the body, and secure each side a cheek of jungle cock substitute. Finally tie in a bunch of orange cock fibres immediately under the eye and sloping well back under the body, and build a good head with the silk.

Dressing

Hook	D/E size 8 long shank
Silk	Black
Tail	Orange cock fibres
Body	Flat gold tinsel or lurex
Rib	Oval gold tinsel
Wing	Bunch of black marabou
Cheeks	Jungle cock substitute
Throat Hackle	Bunch of orange cock hackles

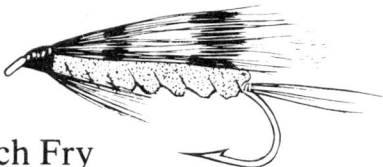

51 The Church Fry

While it is probably true to say that the Jersey Herd was the first lure to be designed specifically for stillwater trout fishing, it was several years after its appearance before lure fishing as we know it today became generally accepted. The Church Fry undoubtedly set the seal on this style of fishing due to its phenomenal success during the 1966 season, after it was popularized in the angling press largely by Dick Walker. This pattern was designed in 1962 by Bob Church to represent a perch fry, at a time when they began to turn up at Ravensthorpe reservoir in increasing numbers, and when there was no satisfactory pattern to represent them. The wing formed from a bunch of hair from a natural grey squirrel tail represented the barred body of the fry very well, but the bright orange body of the lure was completely out of character. Bob explains this very logically, as he felt it was most desirable to present a pattern that would stand out among the natural fry. He chose orange for the body as it seemed to be a particularly attractive colour to trout, and his thinking in this respect most certainly paid off as it has since accounted for many thousands of trout, even in waters where perch fry were absent. Today this lure is still a very popular and killing pattern throughout the season.

To dress this pattern take a long shank hook, and whip the shank with black tying silk down to the bend, where the tail formed from a bunch of white hackle fibres should be tied in. Next tie in a length of silver or gold tinsel for ribbing, followed by the body material of bright orange chenille, which should be wound tightly around the shank nearly up the eye. This is then ribbed with the tinsel and tied off. The throat hackle of a small bunch of crimson dyed hackles is then tied in under the body behind the eye and sloping well back. The wing formed from a substantial bunch of natural grey squirrel tail hair should then be secured on top sloping back over the body beyond the bend. Finally build up a black head from the black tying silk.

Dressing

Hook	D/E size 6 to 10 long shank
Silk	Black
Tail	Bunch of white hackle fibres
Rib	Gold or silver tinsel
Body	Bright orange chenille
Throat Hackle	Crimson dyed hackle fibres
Wing	Bunch of natural grey squirrel tail hair

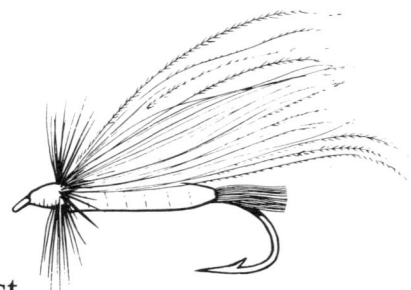

52 Jack Frost

Without doubt this is an excellent name for this new lure, which is the latest creation of Bob Church. It would seem that this is a natural development, following the success of his Appetizer lure which incorporated a relatively new material. This was marabou which he used in conjunction with hair for the wings. The new pattern relies entirely on marabou for the wings, which seems to indicate how very highly Bob thinks of this material. It is so very fine that the slightest movement brings the marabou to life, and for this reason it seems to be more effective fished slowly with frequent pauses, rather than fast. It was first tested at Blagdon during the 1974 season, where it promptly resulted in a limit bag of trout weighing 20lb 4oz. Since then it has proved its worth on many occasions, particularly at Grafham and Pitsford reservoirs where it is now looked upon as an exceptionally good attractor pattern by many of the regulars. The polythene covered body gives it a very translucent effect, so it is an excellent fry imitator for use at the back end of the season.

This is not a difficult lure to dress, but it does take a little time as there are more than the average number of materials involved. Black or white tying silk may be used for this pattern and this should be whipped down the shank to the bend in the normal manner, where the tail of crimson wool is tied in. Follow this with a strip of polythene cut to a width of approximately $\frac{1}{8}$ in. for covering the body. Next tie in a length of white 'Sirdar' brand baby wool to form the body, which should be wound tightly along the shank to the eye. The strip of polythene is then wound over the body up to the eye and tied in. Take a generous spray of white marabou for the wing and tie this in on top behind the eye sloping back over the body and extending well beyond the bend. A long fibred crimson dyed cock hackle should then be wound on behind the eye but in front of the wing, and this should be followed by a long fibred white cock hackle. Both these hackles should be tied well down at the roots so they slope well back down the body.

Dressing

Hook	D/E size 6 to 10 long shank
Silk	Black or white
Tag	Crimson wool
Body	White 'Sirdar' baby wool covered by a $\frac{1}{8}$ in. wide strip of polythene
Wing	Generous spray of white marabou
Hackles	Long fibred crimson cock followed by long fibred white cock

53 The Missionary

This lure is an old, almost forgotten New Zealand pattern, that has been resurrected and brought up to date by that maestro of the stillwater scene Dick Shrive. Due to his astonishing success in recent years with this pattern it has now become extremely popular, particularly on many of the Midland reservoirs. In addition it is highly recommended by Bob Church, so with the backing of two such experts it is obviously worthy of very serious consideration. There are two major variations of this pattern. The first incorporates the use of a whole feather for the wing, tied in flat along the top of the body. This whole feather acts rather like a tiny parachute, so that when the fly is cast on the water it sinks slowly with a most attractive action. Under certain conditions this seems irresistible to any trout in its vicinity, which results in a lot of takes coming on the drop. Apart from this it is also very effective when retrieved at a medium pace, and it is now looked upon by many anglers as an excellent all season pattern on most waters. The second variation which Bob Church and his friends have found particularly successful has been modified for a much faster retrieve. This has been achieved by replacing the whole wing feather with a bunch of barred teal feathers taken off the quill.

It is a fairly simple and straightforward pattern to dress, and should pose few problems for the average amateur fly dresser. White or black thin silk may be used, and this is wound down the shank to the bend where a bunch of scarlet dyed cock hackle fibres for the tail is tied in at the same time as a length of silver tinsel for ribbing the body. This is white chenille wound thickly along the shank to the eye, followed by the ribbing, and both are secured at the eye. Next take another bunch of scarlet dyed cock hackles and tie these in behind and under the eye, sloping well back. The last and most important operation is to tie in, on top behind the eye, a whole silver mallard breast feather, tying it by the quill so that it lies perfectly flat over and along the top of the body. If silver mallard is not available a barred teal feather makes an ideal substitute.

Dressing

Hook	D/E size 6 to 10 long shank
Silk	White or black
Tail	Bunch of scarlet dyed cock hackle fibres
Throat Hackle	Bunch of scarlet dyed cock hackle fibres
Rib	Silver tinsel
Body	White chenille
Wing	A whole silver mallard breast feather

54 The Muddler Minnow

This is an American pattern which caused quite a sensation in the States when it was first introduced in the early 1960s. The pattern was developed by Don Gapen of the Gapen Fly Company of Minnesota in an attempt to imitate the Cockatush minnow, common in the Nipigon river in Northern Ontario and much loved by the trout. This is a flathead type of minnow and in that area is referred to as a muddler, hence the name of the artificial. An immediate success, the fame of this pattern soon spread right across the States as it was found to be an exceptionally killing fly under practically any conditions even where minnows were entirely absent. Like most successful American inventions it eventually arrived in this country during the latter half of the 1967 season. Within a couple of seasons its fame had spread far and wide as it proved a phenomenal success on most of our larger reservoirs, and even today it is still one of the most popular patterns with out stillwater fly fishers. It is an attractor pattern rather than a lure, and I think its success is probably due to the fact that it is a reasonable general representation of several different forms of aquatic life. While it seems to be effective fished in almost any manner, I have personally found it to be most killing retrieved just under the surface on a slow sink, or sink tip line at a medium to slow pace.

A difficult pattern to dress, it should only be attempted by the experienced fly tyer. Black tying should be used and this is wound down the shank to the bend, where the tail, formed from a small section of turkey wing quill (oak), is

secured. Take a length of flat gold tinsel for the body, tie
in at bend, and wind evenly along the shank for a little over
half its length. The winging material is then tied in immediately in front of the tinsel. This should be a substantial
bunch of grey squirrel tail hair, or for patterns dressed on
large hooks, black and white bucktail fibres, which should
extend beyond the bend of this hook. This should be
flanked on each side by a fairly large section of mottled
(oak) turkey wing feather tied on sloping upwards at 30
degrees. So far the dressing is fairly straightforward, but
the next and final operation is very tricky indeed, namely
tying in the head or shoulders of natural deer hair. This is
spun on to surround the shank, and is flattened and
clipped short at front and tapering longer towards the
back. This spinning technique is fully described in a booklet on fly tying innovations by John Veniard.

Dressing

Hook	D/E size 12 to 1 long shank
Silk	Black
Tail	Small section of turkey wing quill (oak) slightly longer than the gape of the hook
Body	Flat gold tinsel
Wing (inner)	Substantial bunch of grey squirrel tail hair or on large hooks black and white bucktail
Wing (outer)	Two large sections of mottled (oak) turkey wing feather
Head	Natural deer hair spun on shank and clipped

55 The Polystickle

A popular and very killing pattern developed by that
master angler Richard Walker. I think it would be right to
say this is one pattern that was developed in the true sense
of the word rather than invented. Dick first described his
stickle patterns in an article in *Trout and Salmon* magazine
in November 1966. They were intended to represent minnows or small fish, the bodies were formed from floss silk
in various colours to the appropriate shape, and backed
with a strip of feather fibre, tied so that a section was left

protruding beyond the bend and trimmed to represent the tail of a fish. Over the years the original shape or silhouette has changed little, but the reverse is true of the materials used. The body is now wonderfully translucent and is formed from stretched polythene, first introduced by Ken Sinfoil in an article in *Angling Times*. A short while after this Dick discovered a brand new material called 'raffene', a synthetic version of raffia, which seemed ideal for the back of the stickle, and so it proved. Polystickles will take trout throughout the season, under any conditions or in any depth of water, but they seem to be most effective when retrieved fast. There is no doubt though, they are most efficient when used for the purpose for which they were designed—to imitate fry. They are particularly deadly fished in or near the margins of the lakes or reservoirs in July and August when the fry are mature enough to leave the shallows for slightly deeper water. As polystickles are so popular they are on general sale in shops, and like Joseph's coat they are supplied in many colours. This was never intended by the originator (of the Polystickle). The following dressing is the only and correct one apart from a variation suggested for fishing at dusk which incorporates a body formed from white D.F. wool but still covered with polythene.

Although it is not a particularly difficult pattern to dress, it may take a little time to perfect the best method of tying the materials to obtain a good silhouette. Take a silvered long shank hook and with black tying silk tie in at the bend a length of brown raffene leaving half an inch or so to project beyond the bend from which to form the tail. The black tying silk is then wound up the shank in open spirals two thirds of the way, where a piece of crimson floss silk is tied in. This is then wound up to the eye and tied off. Next take a long strip of polythene between 0.003in. and 0.005in. thick and secure behind the eye. Wind this round the shank back and forth, pulling the polythene to stretch it when you change direction at each end of the fish shape body you are building up. When the body is fat enough tie in the polythene at the eye and cut off the waste. The hot orange throat hackle of dyed cock fibres is then tied in under the eye, sloping well back. Now thoroughly damp the raffene, stretch firmly over the body to form the back and tie off at the eye. The other end at the bend can then be cut off square to form an imitation fish tail. The last operation is to build up a substantial head from the black tying silk and give it several coats of cellulose varnish.

Dressing

Hook	D/E silver size 6 or 8 long shank
Silk	Black
Body	Shank ribbed black silk two thirds of distance to eye where a length of crimson floss silk is wound in up to eye. This is then covered and built into fish shape body with polythene strip
Throat Hackle	Hot orange dyed cock hackle fibres
Back and tail	Brown raffene
Head	Black tying silk given several coats cellulose

56 The Persuader

This is one of my most recent patterns, and although I designed it for fishing Hanningfield reservoir it has since proved to be a very killing artificial on every water I have fished. In 1975 I provided an article for *Trout and Salmon* magazine and gave the dressing for this new pattern. Since then I have received constant reports concerning its fish-catching qualities. This is an attractor nymph rather than a lure, as I designed it to meet the following requirements: (a) to have a fairly large size in order to attract the attentions of a trout from a reasonable distance; (b) to have an attractive colour or colour combination; and (c) to display a juicy, succulent-looking body. Finally I wanted, if possible, a pattern that would at least loosely resemble some of the more common forms of food on which trout feed. The result after much experimentation turned out as follows. White and orange for the two basic colours, since over the years dressings in either of these have proved exceptionally effective. I decided on white ostrich herl for the main body, as this material is particularly translucent, and for a similar reason I used seal's fur of an orange colour for the thorax. The hook chosen was a long shank size 8 or 10, and for silhouette I settled on a shape which vaguely simulated a sedge pupa. I found that there were two particularly effective methods of fishing the new fly.

Either on a sinking line fished slowly, as near to the bed of the reservoir as possible—this proved very good for the larger browns. Alternatively, retrieved fairly fast just below the surface on a floating or sink tip line in fairly shallow water, or over deep water if there were odd fish rising here and there. As many fly fishers have probably discovered this latter method is in itself a very killing way to fish a large number of patterns. In spite of this it is a technique which few writers to my knowledge have emphasized. I would also add that it has also accounted for a lot of trout when fished on the drop, i.e. cast out over deepish water on a floating line, when the fish will often take it very confidently as it is slowly sinking.

This is a very simple and quick pattern to dress, and is therefore an ideal pattern for the beginner at fly tying. Take a length of orange tying silk and wind down the hook shank to the bend. There secure a length of round silver tinsel for ribbing the body. Next tie in the body material of five strands of white ostrich herl and wind these two thirds of the way along the shank, followed by the silver ribbing, and tie off. The orange seal's fur is then spun on the silk, and wound onto the shank in front of the body material to form the thorax. The wing pads, composed of three strands of dark brown dyed turkey, are then secured on top in front of the eye and doubled and redoubled over the top of the thorax. Finally if the body herl is a little too long trim off to appropriate length with scissors.

Dressing

Hook	D/E size 8 or 10 long shank
Tying silk	Orange
Body	Five strands of white ostrich herl (trim after tying)
Thorax	Orange seal's fur
Rib	Round silver tinsel no. 20
Wing Pads	Three strands of dark brown dyed turkey herl from tail feather

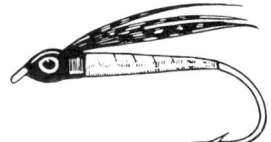

57 Sinfoil's Fry

The inventor of this fine pattern was Mr. Kenneth Sinfoil,

head bailiff of Weir Wood reservoir for many years. It would appear he was the first person to make use of polythene for the bodies of flies, but since then many fly tyers have emulated him and produced similar dressings. I think, however, that his fry pattern is still the best dressing available to represent the immature or very young fry of various species of coarse fish. At this age their bodies are almost transparent, and the polythene body of his pattern simulates them to perfection. In reservoirs or lakes where coarse fish are indigenous, it should be used when trout are feeding on the tiny fry. This usually occurs in the shallows, during late May, June or July. At this time it is best to fish this artificial on a floating line and cast along the bank when fishing from the shore, or in towards the bank from a boat. The retrieve should be fairly fast and it should be fished where trout are observed harrying the fry shoals.

If the following method of dressing is observed, little difficulty should be experienced. Tie in black silk at the eye, but do not wind down the shank. Secure a length of flat silver tinsel, and wind evenly down the shank for two thirds of its length, bring back over itself and tie off a little short of the eye. Take an $\frac{1}{8}$ in. wide strip of 250 gauge polythene and secure with the silk behind the eye. This should then be stretched and wound backwards and forwards over the underbody of tinsel until a smooth carrot shaped effect is achieved. Next wind on a collar of scarlet floss silk about $\frac{1}{8}$ in. wide around the body a short distance back from the eye, ensuring that sufficient room is left to form the rather bulky head. A slim strip of mallard feather is now tied in on top of this to lay flat along the top of the body. The head is now built up to a fairly large size with the black silk, and the final operation is to add a small circle of white paint or varnish on each side to represent the eyes.

Dressing

Hook	D/E size 8 to 12 long shank
Silk	Black
Underbody	Flat silver tinsel
Overbody	$\frac{1}{8}$ in. wide strip of 250 gauge polythene
Collar	Scarlet floss silk
Wing	The 'bad' side of a brown mallard feather
Head	Black tying silk

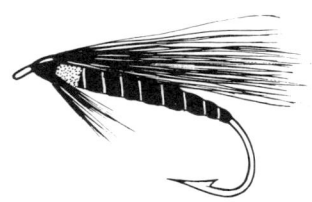

58 Sweeny Todd

This pattern was designed by Richard Walker and Peter Thomas and first introduced to the angling public in the mid 1960s when it was given the somewhat unusual name listed above. It quickly became a firm favourite with still-water fly fishers, and it is even today looked upon as an excellent general lure pattern. It was developed from one of the oldest known fly patterns described in a supplement of Charles Cotton's to Walton's *Compleat Angler*, combining black and silver. Since then a number of effective patterns have been evolved with these basic colours. They include the Black Pennell, Zulu and Black Lure, so this new artificial was really a natural extension of these, incorporating the use of more modern materials. The original pattern was altered considerably before it was finally accepted by both its originators, when it was duly named.

It is a very useful pattern as it can be fished throughout the season, and will take trout under most conditions and, furthermore, retrieved at varying speeds or depths. Reports seem to indicate that the trout are sometimes fussy about the size, so it would seem desirable to carry a range dressed on hook sizes from 14 down to 6. In addition a tandem pattern dressed on two size 8 hooks has proved very effective. Where rules limit hook sizes, this can be overcome fairly successfully by extending the length of the wing to up to twice the length of the hook.

This pattern is freely available in most tackle shops, but it should be noted that many of these dressings are incorrect as they incorporate the use of magenta for the throat hackle, whereas the authors of the pattern are adamant that crimson should be used. To dress, wind black tying silk down the shank to the bend, where a length of fine silver wire is secured for ribbing. The body material composed of black floss silk is then wound two thirds of the distance up the shank and this is followed by the rib and tied in. A short collar of neon magenta D.F. wool is then wound on nearly up to the eye, where the throat hackle of dyed crimson cock fibres is tied in underneath and sloping well back. Finally tie in on top of the hook immediately behind the eye a substantial bunch of black squirrel fibres slightly longer than the hook and sloping well back.

Dressing

Hook	D/E size 6 to 14 long shank
Silk	Black
Rib	Fine silver wire
Body	Black silk floss with collar of neon magenta D.F. wool at wing root
Throat Hackle	Fibres of crimson dyed cock
Wing	Black squirrel

59 The Whisky Fly

Designed by the well known and respected casting coach Albert Whillock in the early 1970s for fishing Hanningfield, his local reservoir, this lure very quickly gained a reputation for catching large trout. Within a comparatively short time its fame spread, and apart from proving to be a very successful pattern on most waters in the UK it is now popular in many other countries, particularly in Canada where it enjoys a great reputation. During the last two seasons it has accounted for seven rainbows over 8lb, and furthermore has also taken the record rainbows from Grafham, Hanningfield, Latimer, Packington, Damerham and Bickton Mill. This would certainly seem to confirm its reputation as a big fish fly at least for rainbows.

An excellent general pattern it seems effective fished at any speed and at any depth, and while it will take trout throughout the season, it is reputed to be most effective during the latter half of the season.

Although it is not a particularly difficult artificial to dress, some little time may be required to obtain the correct materials as some are a little unusual. Start with orange tying silk which is wound down the shank to the bend, where a length of D.R.F. scarlet nylon floss is secured. This is then wound around the shank at this point to form a collar or tag about ⅛ in. long, leaving sufficient hanging down to rib the body. A strip of silver sellotape cut about ⅛ in. wide is then secured with the silk and wound tightly up the shank and tied in a little short of the eye. The scarlet floss is then ribbed along the body and secured and a coat of varnish should be applied over the body and rib. The throat hackle of hot orange cock fibres is then tied in under and behind the eye and sloping well back. Next take a substantial bunch of calf's tail hair dyed hot orange, which should be tied in well behind the eye on top sloping back over the body and extending well beyond the bend. Finally tie in another length of D.R.F. scarlet nylon floss with which to form a substantial head immediately behind the eye, whip finish and varnish.

Dressing

Hook	D/E size 6 to 10 long shank
Silk	Orange
Tag or Collar	D.R.F. scarlet nylon floss
Rib	As above
Body	⅛ in. wide strip of silver sellotape varnished over body and rib
Throat Hackle	Hot orange cock
Wing	Hot orange calf's tail
Head	As for Tag

N.B. Wide silver lurex could be used for body, and hot orange bucktail for the wings.

60 The Worm Fly

The origins of this pattern are somewhat obscure, but there seems little doubt that this tandem lure was developed from the red tag, a very popular grayling fly, which was apparently invented in 1850 by a gentleman named Flynn, a well known Teme angler. According to Thomas Clegg, the celebrated Scottish fly dresser, this tandem pattern as we know it today was perfected by one Donald Watson for loch fishing in the Inverness area, during the latter part of the last century. For several years it enjoyed a certain amount of popularity with Scottish loch fishers, where it was fished either as a wet fly on the drift, or semi-dry as bob fly. However, during the first half of this century it seems to have passed into semi-obscurity. I was first introduced to this artificial in 1957 when fishing the then newly-opened Chew Valley lake in Somerset, so it would appear it was about this time that it was beginning to make a come-back. This was about the same period that lure fishing from the bank as we know it today was becoming very popular. By 1960 this pattern together with the Jersey Herd were looked upon as THE two basic lure patterns, and there is no doubt that for some time they both accounted for a lot of trout. I do not know how it received the name Worm Fly, as I am certain it was never intended to represent a worm or in fact any other specific fauna. On the other hand it does loosely resemble several aquatic species, and this probably accounts for the fact that it seems most effective when retrieved fairly slowly along or near the bottom.

A time-consuming pattern to dress, because you are virtually tying two flies in one. First of all take two size 10 or 12 hooks and join these together about half an inch apart with a length of heavy monofilament or wire. This should be whipped onto each shank with heavy tying silk. Upon completion grip the rear hook in the vice in the normal way and proceed to dress this fly first. Take black tying silk down the shank to the bend where a tag of scarlet wool is secured. Now secure two or three bronze peacock herls, and wind these down the shank nearly to the eye. They should be wound thickening to the shoulder. Finally tie in a fairly long dark red cock or hen hackle sloping well back down the body. Repeat for the front fly but omit the red tag.

Dressing

Tail Fly

Hook   D/E size 10 to 13
Silk   Black
Tag   Scarlet wool or red floss silk
Body   Two or three strands of bronze peacock herl
Hackle Dark red cock or hen

The dressing for the front fly is the same, but without the red tag.